Childre
987
Willis

Willis, Terri.
Venezuela

$40.00

Venezuela

Venezuela

By Terri Willis

Enchantment of the World™
Second Series

Children's Press®

An Imprint of Scholastic Inc.

New York   Toronto   London   Auckland   Sydney
Mexico City   New Delhi   Hong Kong
Danbury, Connecticut

Frontispiece: Canaima National Park

Consultant: Daniel Hellinger, Professor of Political Science and International Relations, Webster University, Webster Groves, Missouri

Please note: All statistics are as up-to-date as possible at the time of publication.

Book production by The Design Lab

Cataloging-in-Publication data is available from the Library of Congress.
ISBN: 978-0-531-25604-6

Venezuela

Contents

Cover photo:
Parachutists at
Angel Falls

Bolívar Peak

Jabiru stork

Resilient, Passionate, Proud

THE PEOPLE OF VENEZUELA ARE RESILIENT. Venezuelans have seen the fortunes of their nation change many times. Thanks to oil, the country has been fabulously wealthy for a time, but for much of its history it has been painfully poor. It has been under the control of Spain and dictators, but now it is being led by a president elected by the people. Some Venezuelans have faith in their government and think it can help solve their problems. Others see the government as the problem.

The people of Venezuela are passionate.

They take certain matters very seriously. Venezuelans have strong religious beliefs but express their spirituality in ways that are all their own. They are huge sports fans and love baseball more than soccer, though soccer is the sport many South Americans enjoy the most. When they speak, they're expressive. They'll wave their arms in anger, and just as quickly, clap their hands together with joy.

The people of Venezuela are proud.

Opposite: **The average woman in Venezuela lives seventy-seven years.**

Resilient, Passionate, Proud **9**

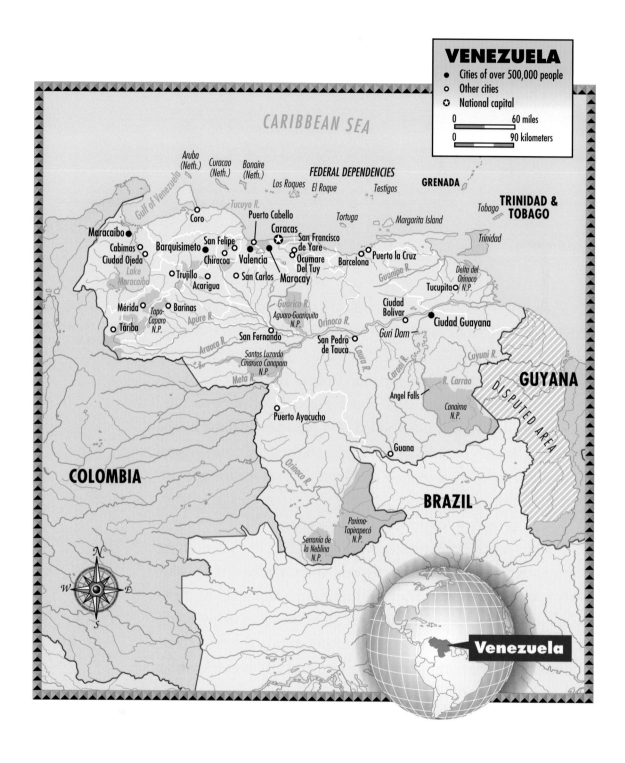

CARIBBEAN SEA

VENEZUELA

● Cities of over 500,000 people
○ Other cities
✪ National capital

0 — 60 miles
0 — 90 kilometers

Aruba
(Neth.)
Curacao
(Neth.)
Bonaire
(Neth.)

FEDERAL DEPENDENCIES

Los Roques   El Roque   Testigos   **GRENADA**

Tortuga   Tobago   **TRINIDAD & TOBAGO**

Margarita Island

Gulf of Venezuela

Coro   Puerto Cabello   *Trinidad*

Tucuyo R.

Maracaibo   San Felipe   **Caracas**

Barquisimeto   San Francisco de Yare

Cabimas   Chiracoa   Valencia   Ocumare Del Tuy   Puerto la Cruz

Ciudad Ojeda   Barcelona

Lake Maracaibo   Trujillo   San Carlos   Maracay

Acarigua   Guanipa R.

Delta del Orinoco N.P.

Mérida   Barinas   Guárico R.   Tucupita

Tapo-Caparo N.P.   Apure R.   Aguaro-Guariquito N.P.   Orinoco R.

Táriba   Ciudad Bolívar

San Fernando   San Pedro de Tauca   Guri Dam   Ciudad Guayana

Arauca R.   Caura R.

Santos Luzardo Cinaruco Canaparo N.P.   Cuyuni R.

Meta R.   Caroní R.   R. Carrao   **GUYANA**

Angel Falls   DISPUTED AREA

Canaima N.P.

COLOMBIA   Puerto Ayacucho

Orinoco R.   Guana

BRAZIL

Parima-Tapirapecó N.P.

Serranía de la Neblina N.P.

N
W   E
S

Venezuela

Venezuelans love their families and work hard to provide for them. Appearance is taken seriously in Venezuela, and poverty is not an excuse for not looking one's best. It's not an excuse for a lack of hospitality, either. Guests are greeted warmly, with as much generosity as the host can afford.

Resilient. Passionate. Proud. Of course these are generalities and don't apply to all Venezuelans, but they do describe the majority of them. The people of Venezuela have many shared experiences and values that give their country a strong national character.

Most families in Venezuela have two or three children.

Boundless Beauty

THE NATURAL BEAUTY OF VENEZUELA SEEMS BOUNDLESS. The country boasts a stunning variety of landscapes. There are the towering peaks of the Andes Mountains, the white sands of the long Caribbean coastline, the Orinoco River and its glistening waterfalls, the vast grasslands of the country's interior, and thick, colorful rain forests.

This country, so rich in diversity, is located at the northern end of South America. Colombia lies to the west of Venezuela, Brazil is to the south, and Guyana is to the east. More than three hundred islands and keys are part of Venezuela, too, although most are tiny. Only Margarita Island is large enough to maintain a sizable population.

Venezuela stretches across 352,143 square miles (912,050 square kilometers), making it about twice the size of California. More than twenty-nine million people live in Venezuela. Most people live in the crowded coastal areas, while much of the interior is lightly populated.

Roraima Tepui rises above the clouds in southeastern Venezuela.

Venezuela's Geographic Features

Area: 352,143 square miles (912,050 sq km)

Length of Coastline: About 1,700 miles (2,800 km)

Highest Elevation: Bolívar Peak, 16,342 feet (4,981 m) above sea level

Lowest Elevation: Sea level along the coast

Longest River: Orinoco, 1,590 miles (2,560 km) long

Largest Lake: Maracaibo, 5,150 square miles (13,300 sq km)

Largest Island: Margarita Island, 394 square miles (1,020 sq km)

Highest Average Temperature: 85°F (29°C) in Maracaibo

Lowest Average Temperature: 65°F (18°C) in Caracas.

Average Annual Precipitation: 33 inches (84 cm) in Caracas; 23 inches (58 cm) in Maracaibo

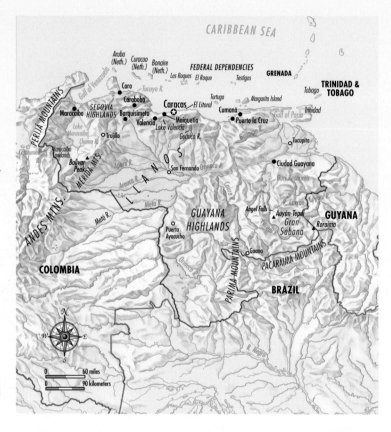

The Andes

The Andes Mountains stretch up the west coast of South America and into northwestern Venezuela. In Venezuela, the Andes divide into two branches, the Perijá and Mérida ranges. The Perijá Mountains run along the border with Colombia. The Mérida Mountains lay farther to the south and east. They include Venezuela's highest point, Bolívar Peak, which reaches a height of 16,342 feet (4,981 meters). One of the largest cities in the Venezuelan Andes is Mérida, with a population of 345,589. Located atop a plateau along the Chama River, it is near some of the Andes's highest peaks.

Rocky Bolívar Peak towers over the city of Mérida.

Thick forests reach to the clouds on the mountains near the coast.

The Segovia Highlands are also part of the Andes region. These highlands are an important agricultural area, their low hills and plains supporting sugar and cacao plantations. Copper was discovered there in 1605, and some mining still goes on. Barquisimeto, Venezuela's fourth-largest city, was founded here as a mining community.

The Coastal Region

Venezuela's coastal region is thin. Tall mountains, thick with forests, dominate the landscape not far inland. In many places, the coast is only a few miles wide. Because it was difficult for Spanish explorers to travel over the mountains, most of their early settlements were on the coast. Many of these have developed into modern cities. Though the coastal region covers only 3 percent of the country, it is Venezuela's most densely populated area. Caracas, Venezuela's capital, is one of the many coastal cities.

The coast is lined with beaches, making it popular with tourists. A popular destination is Mochima National Park, which has white sand beaches and great waters for snorkeling and scuba diving. Margarita Island, Venezuela's largest island, has several cities and is the country's top vacation destination.

The Maracaibo Lowlands

In the northwest of the country, between the Mérida and Perijá ranges, is a region called the Maracaibo Lowlands. It is one of the hottest areas in South America, with an average year-round temperature of 82 degrees Fahrenheit (28 degrees Celsius).

Mochima National Park is known for its quiet beaches, calm waters, and rugged cliffs.

There is little wind there to take the edge off the heat, because the mountains block the blow of air from the Pacific.

This region gets its name from Lake Maracaibo, the largest lake in South America. The lake is about 133 miles (214 km) long and 75 miles (120 km) wide at its maximum points. It covers an area nearly the size of the U.S. state of Connecticut. A narrow strait connects Lake Maracaibo to the Gulf of Venezuela in the Caribbean Sea. During high tide, ships can pass through the strait.

Long before Europeans arrived in the region, native people built houses on stilts along the shore of Lake Maracaibo. Today, many houses still sit above the lapping water.

Venezuela's Largest Cities

Caracas, the capital of Venezuela, is the nation's largest city, with a population of about 6,000,000. Maracaibo, with a population of 1,891,800 residents, is the nation's second-largest city. Located well inland on the shores of Lake Maracaibo, the city has a hot climate and can become nearly a ghost town in the middle of the day, when the sun is at its highest point in the sky. People go home to rest in their air-conditioning before returning to their jobs for the early evening. Maracaibo is one of Venezuela's wealthiest cities. Before the oil boom started, Maracaibo was a quiet village. But when the demand for oil shot up in the 1920s, so did the city's income. Today, it remains at the center of Venezuela's oil economy and an important port. The city had been isolated from the rest of Venezuela for hundreds of years, as Lake Maracaibo was difficult to travel around. This changed in 1962, with the comple-

tion of the Rafael Urdaneta Bridge (left), built across the strait that links the lake to the Caribbean Sea. At 5.4 miles (8.7 km) it is South America's longest bridge.

Valencia (above), in the northern part of the country, has 1,408,400 residents, making it Venezuela's third-largest city. Founded in 1555, it boasts many old buildings that have been restored. Today, it is a booming industrial city. Valencia's Aquarium, the largest aquarium in Latin America, also has a small zoo, and together they showcase many of Venezuela's native animals.

Barquisimeto is Venezuela's fourth-largest city. It is home to 1,018,900 people, and the popular belief is that nearly all of them play a musical instrument. While that is an exaggeration, Barquisimeto does have a reputation as Venezuela's musical capital. In addition to listening to live music played in parks and plazas throughout the city, tourists can visit the city's many museums that showcase history, archaeology, and paleontology.

Vast oil deposits lie beneath Lake Maracaibo. They were discovered in the early 1900s, and today thousands of wells churn along the lake's eastern shore. Thousands more rise above the surface of the lake.

The Llanos Region

The *llanos*, or plains, cover the vast Orinoco River valley in central and eastern Venezuela. These low-lying grasslands are 600 miles (1,000 km) long and 200 miles (320 km) wide, stretching over about one-third of the country. The many streams and rivers that flow through the llanos frequently flood during the rainy winter season, which lasts from May to October. Drought is common during the dry summer months of November to April.

Mighty River

The Orinoco River and its many tributaries make up the third-largest river system in South America. The Orinoco flows for 1,590 miles (2,560 km), all of it in Venezuela. It begins as a mountain stream in the rain forest of the Parima range, along Venezuela's border with Brazil. From there, it flows northeast, adding water from many tributaries in the llanos before emptying into the Atlantic Ocean.

The Orinoco is an average of 4 miles (6 km) wide, and deep enough for oceangoing ships to travel on it for about 260 miles (420 km) from its mouth to the city of Ciudad Bolívar. Smaller boats can travel as far as 1,000 miles (1,600 km) upriver.

The soil in the llanos is poor and not good for growing crops, but many ranches are located there. Most of Venezuela's 16.7 million cattle are raised in the llanos. In recent years, dams have been built in the llanos to control flooding and provide irrigation. These projects have made it possible to grow corn and rice in the llanos.

Venezuelan cowboys round up cattle on the llanos.

The Guiana Highlands

The Guiana Highlands, located in southeastern Venezuela, make up nearly half the nation. Natural resources in the region include forests, iron ore, bauxite, gold, and diamonds.

Ciudad Bolívar, one of the region's main cities, has a bustling port. Large amounts of steel and aluminum are shipped from there, along the Orinoco River to the Atlantic Ocean.

In the Gran Sabana, abrupt rock formations rise from the broad grasslands.

The Gran Sabana (the great savannah), south of Ciudad Bolívar, is an unusual landscape dominated by formations called *tepuis*. These are flat-topped mountains, with sheer cliffs rising from the forest floor. British author Sir Arthur Conan Doyle, who wrote the Sherlock Holmes mysteries, visited the Gran Sabana. The mysterious landscape inspired him to write a novel called *The Lost World*, about prehistoric creatures that have come back to life.

The top of the largest tepui, Auyán-Tepui, covers 270 square miles (700 sq km). Angel Falls, the world's highest waterfall, rushes down its side for 3,212 feet (979 m). This falls is more than twice the height of Chicago's Willis Tower (formerly the Sears Tower), the tallest building in North America. When water leaves the top of Angel Falls, it drops for fourteen seconds before it lands. The tallest tepui in the Gran Sabana, at 9,219 feet (2,810 m), is Roraima, located near the border with Brazil and Guyana.

Climate

Venezuela lies in the tropics, the band of the earth that is halfway between the North and the South Poles. The temperatures in tropical areas don't vary much over the course of the year. But different parts of Venezuela typically have very different temperatures. This is mostly caused by differences in elevation. On the peaks of the Andes, snow covers the ground year-round. Most places with elevations above 6,600 feet (2,000 m) have average temperatures of 48°F to 52°F (9°C to 11°C). At elevations

Angel Falls

The world's highest waterfall, Angel Falls, was hidden away for centuries from all but the native people living near Auyán-Tepui. In 1910, Ernesto Sánchez La Cruz, a Venezuelan explorer, spotted it and introduced it to the rest of the world. The waterfall gets its name from

Jimmie Angel, an American pilot who first landed atop Auyán-Tepui in 1921 with a gold prospector. On a return trip in 1937 his plane crashed into the boggy tepui surface near the falls, and got stuck there. He and his passengers survived, but they had to trek eleven days through dense jungle and climb down the steep cliffs before reaching a village.

Angel Falls is located within Venezuela's Canaima National Park, one of the six largest national parks in the world, and the second largest in Venezuela. Modern tourists can still fly over Angel Falls to view it, but clouds sometimes block the view. Since there are no roads to the falls, the only other way to get to its base is by a long but interesting journey by plane, on foot, and by boat. These tours take three days and two nights.

Catatumbo Lightning

There is only one place on Earth that experiences the strange phenomenon known as Catatumbo lightning. For ten hours a night, lightning flashes almost constantly over the mouth of the Catatumbo River, where it empties into Lake Maracaibo. Catatumbo lightning occurs about 150 nights a year.

The exact cause of the lightning is unknown. Many scientists believe that when the hot, moist air blowing across the lake and plains collides with cold air from the Andes Mountains, it creates electrical charges.

Others say methane gas released by nearby marshes fuels the lightning displays.

Catatumbo lightning was first described in print in a poem written in 1597. It has occurred regularly for centuries, though mysteriously, it stopped completely in January 2010. Those who feared it had ended permanently were relieved when the lightning began making regular appearances again in April of that year. It is possible that drought caused the lightning to stop during this period.

ranging from 2,600 to 6,600 feet (800 to 2000 m), temperatures average between 54°F and 77°F (12°C and 25°C). And at the lowest elevations, the weather is warm, with average temperatures ranging from 79°F to 82°F (26°C to 28°C).

Venezuela has a wet season and a dry season. The trade winds from the northeast bring in dry air from November to April. In the rainy season, from May to October, rains are usually brief, intense downpours in the afternoon, especially in the northern part of the country. The skies quickly clear after the cloudbursts. More rain falls farther south, over the llanos and Guiana Highlands. In this part of the country, about 59 inches (150 cm) of rain falls each year.

Venezuelans huddle under a tarp during a rainstorm in Caracas. Rain falls in the city an average of 115 days a year.

A Land Alive

V ENEZUELA IS A LAND ALIVE. ITS PLAINS AND forests, rivers and coastlines abound with diverse mammals, birds, reptiles, amphibians, fish, and a lot of interesting plants, too.

Mammals

Many of Venezuela's mammal species live in the rain forests in the southeast, including several kinds of predators. There are foxes, bush dogs, spectacled bears, sloths, and wildcats such as pumas, jaguars, and ocelots. Their diets are varied. The common fox, for example, eats mice, doves, iguanas, and mangoes.

Weighing in at as much as 300 pounds (140 kilograms), tapirs are large creatures related to anteaters, horses, and rhinoceroses. They live in Venezuela's forest and jungle areas, and eat grasses and leaves. Their long snouts are highly flexible and can move in all directions, allowing them to get at food that may be hard for other animals to reach. Tapirs that live near rivers often spend a lot of time cooling off in the water.

Capybaras are social animals. They usually live in groups ranging in size from ten to one hundred.

Venezuela is home to the world's largest rodent, the capybara, which can grow to the size of a small pig. Though capybaras typically live on land, they have webbed feet that aid in swimming, so they also get around easily in the water.

Vampire Bats

Many kinds of bats live in Venezuela. Easily the most feared is the vampire bat. This mammal's name comes from the fact that it does, indeed, suck blood from its victims, just like mythical vampires. Vampire bats feed at night. They typically prey on small, sleeping animals. A vampire bat will swoop down on its prey, make a small cut with its teeth, and then drink its victim's blood. Occasionally, vampire bats are infected with rabies and spread the disease when they bite their victims. In 2007 and 2008, vampire bat bites caused an outbreak of rabies in Venezuela. At least thirty-eight Warao Indians living in remote villages in the Orinoco River delta died. Most of them were children.

This makes them well suited for life in the llanos. They feed on grasses, aquatic plants, fruit, and tree bark.

Many dolphins live off Venezuela's coast. These intelligent mammals are well adapted to life in the water. They have strong fins that enable them to move through the water with force and grace.

Another mammal living in the waters of Venezuela is the West Indian manatee. Manatees live in the Maracaibo Lake basin, the Orinoco River, and its delta. These large, gentle creatures swim near the surface so they can easily take breaths of air when needed. Many manatees are accidentally cut by motorboat blades and are in danger of going extinct.

Manatees are large, slow-moving creatures. They feed primarily on plants.

Giant river otters are also in danger of extinction. They have been hunted extensively for their soft, thick fur. In addition, water pollution and deforestation along rivers have harmed their habitats. Only a few thousand river otters remain in the wild.

Birds

Venezuela is a paradise for birds. More than 1,300 species live in the country. Venezuela has more types of birds than the entire continents of North America and Europe combined. Some, such as the velvet-browed brilliant and the peacock coquette, are found nowhere else in the world. Many birds also stop in Venezuela during their migration across South America.

Giant river otters grow up to 6 feet (2 m) long, about twice the length of North American river otters.

The jabiru and maguari storks, the largest birds in Venezuela, are long-legged and showy. They walk across the flooded plains of the llanos hunting for fish.

Twenty-one species of heron have been seen in Venezuela. Known by their straight bills and long legs, herons hold their necks in an S shape while in flight. They, too, move easily across the wet plains, and along swamps and rivers, feeding on fish and crustaceans. Other birds of the llanos include macaws, hawks, egrets, and vultures.

Venezuela hosts more than three hundred types of hummingbirds. These little flying machines have an astonishingly fast wing beat, flapping seventy or more times each second. Because they expend so much energy, they need to eat almost constantly. Hummingbirds usually have bright colors, making them easy to spot as they use their long, sharp beaks to snag insects in midair or sip nectar from flowers.

The jabiru stork is easily identified by the bright red pouch on its neck. These large birds eat fish, shellfish, frogs, mice, bird eggs, and whatever else they can find.

The National Bird

The national bird of Venezuela is the troupial, which has bright yellow feathers accented by black, red, and white. A type of oriole, the troupial lives in woodlands, forests, and grasslands. Its diet consists of insects, fruits, small birds, and eggs. Troupials don't construct their own nests. Instead, they find abandoned nests to use or drive other birds out of nests and settle in those.

Venezuela's rain forest is alive with the sights and sounds of birds. Colorful spotted toucans and parakeets flutter among the branches, looking for food. Macaws add brilliant shades of red, orange, and yellow to the scene.

Along the Venezuelan coast, pelicans, gulls, and other shorebirds are abundant. And above the Andes, condors soar.

Toucans have large, brightly colored beaks.

Reptiles and Amphibians

Venezuela is also home to many reptiles and amphibians. The Orinoco crocodile is the largest predator in all of South America. Adults range from about 10 to 16 feet (3 to 5 m) long and weigh up to 850 pounds (380 kg). Orinoco crocodiles typically live on fish, but they can eat any animal they encounter, such as deer or capybaras. Orinoco crocodiles are critically endangered. Young ones are vulnerable to being eaten by vultures and some large lizards, but the bigger threat comes from humans. From the 1940s to the 1960s, thousands of these crocodiles were slaughtered in the Orinoco River and the llanos. Hunters wanted them for their hide, which was prized for making shoes and handbags. Today, Orinoco crocodiles are protected, but they are still sometimes hunted illegally.

Orinoco crocodiles are endangered. Only a few hundred remain in the wild.

Another species of crocodile, the spectacled caiman, is slightly smaller than the Orinoco crocodile. These creatures often lie still at the water's edge, waiting silently for prey.

More than 142 species of snakes slither through Venezuela. About 25 of these are poisonous, one of which is the rattlesnake. Rattlesnakes usually target small rodents as their prey, thereby helping local farmers protect their crops. A few other snakes can kill by squeezing the life out of their prey. One of these is the anaconda, the world's largest snake. Boa constrictors also live in Venezuela.

Other dangerous animals include poison-arrow frogs. The skin of these creatures, which live south of the Orinoco River, produces a poison. Native people living in the area once used this poison on the tips of their darts and arrows. Poison-arrow frogs tend to be brightly colored. In some species of these frogs, females lay their eggs on the fathers' backs. The eggs remain there until they hatch, and then the tadpoles swim away.

Male or Female?

Female spectacled caimans can lay up to forty eggs at one time. But the young caimans inside the eggs are neither male nor female at this point. The temperature in the nest determines what gender the developing eggs become. Caimans build nests of plants that slowly decay and give off heat, keeping the nest a steady temperature. If the nest is kept at warmer temperatures, the eggs develop into males. Cooler temperatures produce females.

Poison-arrow frogs are brightly colored. Their vivid colors warn predators to stay away.

The arrau sideneck, the largest freshwater turtle in Venezuela, lives along the Orinoco River and its tributaries. This turtle has been hunted extensively as food and is now endangered. Another turtle, the Venezuelan slider, lives only in a small coastal area in the northwest. Fewer than five hundred of these creatures remain. They've been hunted for food, and pollution has damaged their habitat.

Beneath the Water

Abundant fish swim in Venezuela's rivers, lakes, and coastal waters. Red snapper, shrimps, sardines, oysters, clams, and lobsters are plentiful along the Caribbean coast, as are larger

A school of chub swims in Los Roques.

sea creatures, such as swordfish, yellowfin tuna, barracuda, and marlin. Trout live in the streams and lakes of the Andes. In Los Roques, a large marine preserve in the Caribbean, snorkelers and divers can see colorful angelfish, porcupine fish, parrot fish, moray eels, and many other types of sea life.

The National Flower

The orchid is Venezuela's national flower. The country has some 1,200 varieties of this beautiful plant. Orchids come in nearly every shade of white, purple, pink, and red. They grow throughout the country but are especially common in the coastal mountains and the Andes.

The cachama is one of the largest fish of the Orinoco River, weighing up to 40 pounds (18 kg). This black-and-white fish is related to the meat-loving piranha, but the cachama eats only aquatic plants and tiny sea creatures.

Plants

Many plants grow in Venezuela's rain forest, south of the Orinoco. Among the most beautiful are orchids, which have showy, colorful flowers. The orchid named the Superb is indeed just that. It has beautiful lavender flowers edged in deep purple, with a center of yellow and fuchsia.

The cachama is a popular catch for fishers in Venezuela. It is also farmed in large tanks.

Meat-Eating Plants

Many of the plants growing atop the tepuis of the Guiana Highlands are carnivorous, meaning they eat meat. Specifically, these plants eat insects. Carnivorous plants in Venezuela include marsh pitchers (right) and bladderworts. Most meat-eating plants have flowers shaped like deep bowls. These collect rainwater, which in turn attracts insects. The insects often become trapped in the bowls and die. Through their leaves, the plants absorb nutrients from the decaying insects. This allows the plants to get nutrition, even when they are growing in poor soil.

Heliconia, another rain forest flower, is prized for its beauty. This plant, which can grow to 20 feet (6 m), has sturdy, canoe-shaped leaves that capture rainwater and create miniature pools. In these pools, insects and tiny frogs grow safely to maturity. Giant ferns have been growing in Venezuela's forests for some three hundred million years.

The National Tree

The national tree of Venezuela is the araguaney. This medium-size tree grows throughout the country, in places ranging from grasslands to hillsides to cities. Each year, it produces a massive display of yellow flowers. When the dry season begins, the flowers become even more obvious. The leaves fall away, leaving only the brilliant flowers on the branches. The wood of the araguaney is used to make furniture, and some native people use it for making hunting bows.

Tepuis dominate the landscape in the Guiana Highlands. The climate at the top of tepuis is cool and wet. The tepuis support few animals, but many plants thrive there. Moss and lichen grow well on rock. These small plants help break down the tepui rock, turning it into soil that supports other plants.

Tree ferns are common in Venezuela's rainy forests.

Through the Years

People who grew their own food stayed longer in one place, so they built more permanent shelters and kept larger stores of food. They became healthier, lived longer, and had more children. As the population began to grow, some groups joined together based on similar traditions or languages, or because they lived near one another. Instead of hundreds of diverse groups, a few distinct cultures emerged. The three main groups were the Arawak, the Carib, and the Chibcha.

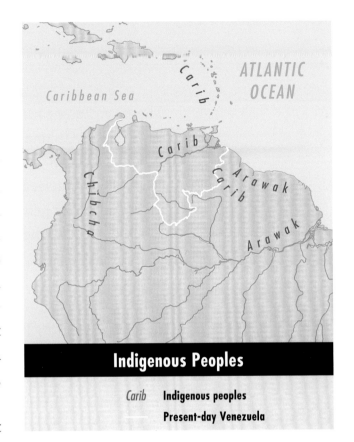

Indigenous Peoples

Carib   **Indigenous peoples**
          Present-day Venezuela

The Arawaks lived throughout much of the llanos and north to the coast. Some farmed, growing vegetables and cotton, though hunting and gathering met the needs of most. The Carib people lived along the central and eastern coasts. Fish were plentiful, and hunting was good there. Fruits and vegetables grew in the wild, but the Caribs also grew their own food.

Most of the Chibcha groups lived in the Andes. The land there did not naturally provide as much food, so they developed more advanced farming techniques. They terraced the hillsides, making flat, level areas on which to grow crops. They learned how to direct water to their fields to irrigate crops, especially potatoes and corn. Different Chibcha groups often worked together, and their settlements were connected by a series of trails.

Europeans Arrive

The first Europeans to visit Venezuela were the explorer Christopher Columbus and his crew, who arrived in 1498. When Columbus landed in the Gulf of Paria, along the east coast of Venezuela, he said the spot was the "loveliest in all the world." The people were friendly, he later wrote, and he was impressed by their jewelry made of pearls and gold.

When other explorers heard of his travels, some were inspired to make the trip to search for gold, pearls, and riches for themselves. Both Amerigo Vespucci and Alonso de Ojeda sailed to Lake Maracaibo and saw reed huts built on stilts in the shallow waters. Reminded of the canals of Venice, Italy, Vespucci named the area *Venezuela*, meaning "little Venice."

More Spaniards arrived in the Americas in the years to come. Following a journey to Mexico, Hernán Cortés brought a huge supply of gold back to Spain. This prompted even more Europeans to travel to the Americas, certain that great wealth was hidden there. Since Venezuela is located at the northeastern tip of South America, it became the most convenient landing place for these explorers.

In 1500, Spaniards founded the island community of Nueva Cádiz, off the coast of Venezuela. This became a hot spot for pearl harvesting. The Spaniards also settled a few places along the Caribbean coast, including Cumaná in 1521, which became the first Spanish town in continental South America.

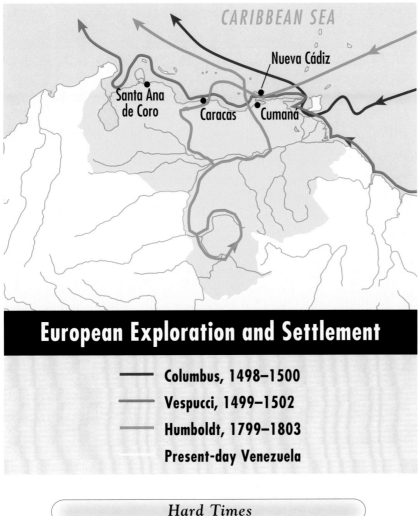

CARIBBEAN SEA

Nueva Cádiz

Santa Ana
de Coro

Caracas Cumaná

European Exploration and Settlement

——— Columbus, 1498–1500

——— Vespucci, 1499–1502

——— Humboldt, 1799–1803

Present-day Venezuela

Hard Times

The arrival of Europeans was devastating for the native people of Venezuela. Spanish slave traders kidnapped villagers and forced them to work. The Europeans stole from the local people and killed them.

The Europeans also introduced deadly diseases into Venezuela. Smallpox had long existed in Europe, so Europeans had developed natural immunities to it. Although the disease would make

The native people of Venezuela sometimes fought the Spanish, trying to drive the newcomers from their land.

them sick, few died from it. But the indigenous, or native, people of Venezuela had never before been exposed to smallpox, so their bodies had no natural defenses. The disease swept through their communities, killing many thousands of people.

After years of mistreatment by the Spaniards, the native people resisted European settlement. Many Spanish expeditions disappeared. In some cases, native people had fought the Spaniards. Other times, the Spaniards were simply unable to survive for long in the rain forest or the desolate llanos.

The Europeans did not give up easily in their quest for gold. They continued exploring Venezuela. By the mid-1500s, however, the Spaniards began to realize that Venezuela probably did not have the gold they had been seeking. But they now wanted something else. They began an effort to colonize the land for Spain. As they moved into the Andes and elsewhere, building roads and towns, they explored much of the great Orinoco River. Spanish colonist Diego de Losada founded Caracas along the northern coast in 1567.

The Spaniards treated the native people cruelly, enslaving many.

By 1600, more than twenty Spanish settlements were scattered across the region, mostly in the Andes and along the coast. Spain now controlled Venezuela.

Colonial Times

The Spanish colonization of Venezuela forever changed it. Spaniards brought in new fruits to grow, such as pomegranates, quinces, and figs. They began to harvest tobacco, coffee, and cacao, which is used to make chocolate. The Europeans also brought in domesticated cattle, and began to raise cows, pigs, sheep, and horses. This expanded into the llanos, and was the start of the country's cattle industry.

Caracas became the capital of Spain's Venezuela Province in 1577.

Harvesting cacao in Venezuela. Cacao trees produce large pods. Inside are seeds that are the main ingredient in chocolate.

The nation's population became more diverse as well, as Spanish settlers had children with the native Indians. Additionally, some Spaniards brought enslaved Africans to Venezuela to work on the coastal plantations. In fact, they brought so many Africans that by the eighteenth century, Africans outnumbered native people in Venezuela. Over time, the native people of Venezuela, the Spaniards, and the Africans had children together, resulting in the great majority of people in Venezuela having mixed ancestry today.

From Continent to Continent

When Spaniards arrived in the Americas, they brought along horses, cattle, chickens, and other animals. All of these animals were new to the Americas, and they had a profound impact on the lives of the people who lived there. Horses made travel faster and hunting easier, and cattle ranching eventually became big business. In time, Europeans also brought wheat, coffee, sugarcane, bananas, and many other crops that would be staples in the Americas.

The flow of new products also went in the other direction. Turkeys were unknown in Europe until they were brought over from the Western Hemisphere. By the mid-1500s, they were a favorite dish at English feasts. Many vegetables that were originally from the Americas changed cultures around the world. Before travel between the hemispheres, there were no potatoes in Ireland or tomatoes in Italy. Peanuts, sweet potatoes, and manioc spread to Africa, where they became important foods. And it was the introduction of chili peppers from the Americas that gave Korean, Thai, and other Asian cuisines their spicy hotness.

The Spaniards held all the power, although they made up only about 20 percent of the population. They did not allow other peoples to attend their churches, be educated in their universities, or even dress in the same style of clothing that they wore.

Venezuela was not as important to the Spanish crown as some other colonies, because it did not have riches. Places such as Bolivia, Colombia, and Peru had greater resources, so Spain focused attention on them. Venezuela was left to develop on its own. With few trading partners around the world, Venezuelans had to supply for themselves everything they needed. People of color and mixed race did most of the labor. Any profits went to the white minority.

In the mid-1700s, a taste for chocolate spread throughout the United States and Europe, and suddenly Venezuela was in the spotlight. Its cacao plantations helped supply the growing demand for chocolate. Plantation owners quickly grew wealthy. Caracas became a center of economic activity. As Venezuela's influence grew, Spain gave it greater political and military authority. It was becoming a very important colony.

The Fight for Independence

The native and mixed-race people of Venezuela were angry at the little control they had over their own lives. They were willing to fight for their freedom. When the French army occupied Spain in 1810, the king lost his power, throwing the country into turmoil. It was time for Venezuelans to make their move. Spain had too many problems at home

Santa Ana de Coro

The first capital of Venezuela was Santa Ana de Coro, founded in 1527. Today, it is the oldest city in western Venezuela and is included on the United Nations' World Heritage list as having outstanding cultural significance. Santa Ana de Coro, commonly known as Coro, features cobblestone streets with some six hundred restored colonial-era homes and other buildings.

Coro was a busy jumping-off point for expeditions searching for gold. Over time, however, Caracas passed Coro as the center of activity in Venezuela. Several times in its history, Coro was raided by pirates. Today, Coro's problems come from weather. The clay adobe that was used to construct the historic buildings is beginning to fail after centuries of rain and wind. In 2005, Coro was officially listed as an "endangered" World Heritage site.

to pay attention to what was happening in Venezuela. Led by Francisco de Miranda, a native of Caracas, the rebelling Venezuelans ousted their Spanish rulers in 1811. In 1812, Miranda became dictator of Venezuela.

From the start, Miranda faced problems. His government had little structure and meager funds. Other Venezuelans, troops made up of a mixed-race underclass, wanted to oust him. The Spanish governor offered land and freedom to the poor, while Miranda and other upper-class Venezuelans wanted to keep the economy and society the way they were. Miranda stepped down after a few months. Spain regained control.

Some of Miranda's closest advisers quickly left Venezuela. Among them was a young man named Simón Bolívar. In 1813, he returned to Venezuela along with the small army he had gathered. Bolívar and his troops began what they called a "War to the Death" against the Spaniards. They recaptured Caracas, and Bolívar was called *El Libertador*, the liberator of his country.

Simón Bolívar played a vital role in helping Venezuela achieve independence from Spain. He also led Bolivia, Colombia, Ecuador, and Peru to independence.

Simón Bolívar (on white horse) greets the victorious soldiers after the Battle of Carabobo.

Bolívar faced opposition from some Venezuelans, though. The *llaneros*, a fierce band of horsemen from the llanos, had been promised land and freedom in return for fighting for the Spanish king. They forced Bolívar out of the country again. But he

The Battle of Carabobo

The Battle of Carabobo is celebrated in Venezuela each year on June 24, often with elaborate parades showing off the country's military might.

That military might was in full force on June 24, 1821, when the Venezuelan troops, struggling for their independence, learned that Spanish soldiers were advancing on the city of Caracas. Simón Bolívar and José Antonio Páez, leaders of the revolutionary army, had a plan. They led 7,500 troops into battle in the southwest part of Valencia, on the plains of Carabobo. These troops included many horsemen from the llanos. The fierce fighting against 5,000 Spanish soldiers lasted little more than one hour. The Venezuelans were victorious. The battle ensured Venezuela's independence.

returned in 1817 with a plan to bring the llaneros to his side. He would work with them to take over the ranches and plantations owned by Spaniards and then divide that land among the llaneros. The plan worked. In 1819, Bolívar was elected president of the Republic of Gran Colombia, as Venezuela was then known. Though Spain still controlled a small portion of the country, the Battle of Carabobo in June 1821 put an end to that. After eleven years of fighting, during which nearly a quarter of its people were killed, Venezuela was now free.

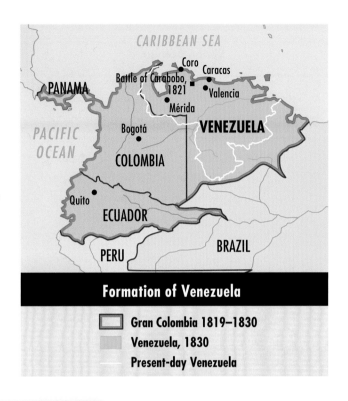

Formation of Venezuela

Gran Colombia 1819–1830
Venezuela, 1830
Present-day Venezuela

Free at Last

Bolívar next set his sights on a grander ideal: to unify Venezuela with the area that is now Colombia, Ecuador, and Panama. He imagined it as an independent state to be called Gran Colombia. Eventually, Bolívar believed that all of Latin America could be united as the world's largest country. He left Venezuela for several years to help speed the process. In his absence, unrest brewed back home. Many people in Venezuela did not want to join the huge nation of Bolívar's dream. Bolívar also lost support because, while he generally wanted to keep the promise of giving the llaneros land and freedom, the upper classes did not. Bolívar returned in 1828 to try to resolve the problems, but he was unable to. He gave up power in 1830 and died in December of that year.

Simón Bolívar

Simón Bolívar is the most respected historical figure in Venezuela. It would be difficult to overstate the importance of his efforts in forming the nation. He brought independence not only to Venezuela but also to Colombia, Panama, Ecuador, Peru, and Bolivia, helping free all of them from Spanish rule. Yet Bolívar was never able to achieve his greatest dream, uniting all of South America into one large country.

Bolívar was born in Caracas on July 24, 1783. His wealthy family had lived in Venezuela for two hundred years. Both his parents died while he was young. He inherited a great fortune and was raised by an uncle, who hired him private tutors and sent him to Europe at

age sixteen to continue his education. It was there that he developed many of his ideas about freedom. As a young man, he met with leaders of the French Revolution. He also traveled to the United States to observe the young country following its own revolution. When he returned to Venezuela, he was fully inspired to lead his countrymen in their own fight for freedom.

By all accounts, he was a great leader, inspiring his troops on to great victories for more than a decade. After years of struggle to free so many South American nations from Spanish rule, Bolívar set his sights on bringing them together under one flag. A united South America, he believed, would be the most powerful nation in the world. But there were too many different cultures, too many different problems and ideas. It proved an impossible task. He was nearly assassinated for his efforts.

For all his success, Bolívar died a depressed and bitter man, feeling like a failure. He was forty-seven.

A New Independence

Venezuela was now an independent nation. Its first president was General José Antonio Páez, who ruled from 1830 to 1835 and then again from 1839 to 1843. He worked to stabilize the country after many years of war. Roads and bridges were rebuilt, the economy grew stronger, and there was order despite rebellions that sprang up. Even when Páez was no longer president, he remained politically influential until 1849. The tide turned against him at that point, after he led failed rebellions against the sitting president. Páez was exiled in 1850, became dictator of Venezuela from 1861 to 1863, and then was exiled again.

As a boy, José Antonio Páez was a ranch hand. He later owned land and cattle and became a leader of the llaneros.

Alexander von Humboldt

In Caracas, an avenue, a university, and a school are all named after a German scientist named Alexander von Humboldt. But why?

Humboldt was the first person to study and record in a modern scientific manner many of Venezuela's natural resources—its plants, animals, and minerals. His journey to Venezuela came about as a fortunate accident. Humboldt had originally planned to join an expedition that was circling the globe, but that trip was postponed. Then he hoped to accompany Napoléon Bonaparte, the leader of France, on a scientific expedition to Egypt, but he had no way to get there. So he went to Madrid, Spain, instead, where he had a chance meeting with an associate of the king of Spain. He was encouraged to make the trip to Latin America.

On July 16, 1799, Humboldt landed at Cumaná, Venezuela. He explored the valleys of Caracas and Lake Valencia, the llanos, and then the entire length of the Orinoco River. He also explored Venezuela's largest cave, which is now named for him.

Throughout his explorations, he carefully observed the natural world around him, as well as many native people and their cultures, and documented his findings. He wrote of the llanos, "All around us the plains seemed to ascend to the sky, and the vast and profound solitude appeared like an ocean covered with seaweed." Humboldt also wrote about crocodiles he observed in the Orinoco that were 24 feet (7 m) long. They "swarm like worms in the shallow waters of the river," he wrote. Humboldt captured electric eels to observe them more closely and got some dangerous shocks from them.

After his time in Venezuela, Humboldt also explored Colombia, Ecuador, Peru, and Mexico before finally returning to Europe in 1804. He became a popular writer and speaker, discussing his many scientific findings until his death in 1859.

A man sells bread from his mule on the streets of Caracas. By 1900, the city was home to about one hundred thousand people.

The decades leading up to the twentieth century were violent in Venezuela. There were dictatorships, revolts, and civil war. Power changed hands many times, but it always remained within the white elite community. Some good things happened, though. Slavery was abolished. Museums were built. Free public education was established, although most children still did not go to school. Caracas became increasingly modern.

Oil wells rise above the waters of Lake Maracaibo in 1935. More than ten thousand wells were eventually drilled in the lake.

The Oil Rush

In Venezuela, people had long known there was oil under the ground. Native people used the sticky black goo to help waterproof their canoes. In the early twentieth century, with the invention of the automobile, people were suddenly clamoring for oil.

Venezuela was in a position to meet the demand. In 1922, a Venezuelan division of Shell Oil, exploring near Lake Maracaibo, drilled a well that pumped out some one hundred thousand barrels of oil each day. Money was pouring into the country. Venezuela quickly became a wealthy nation.

More wells were dug, and people hurried in from other nations seeking work. Many Venezuelans also joined the oil industry, leaving their jobs in ranching, agriculture, and manufacturing.

With few workers left, these industries dried up. Venezuela now had to use its new riches to purchase necessary goods from elsewhere. Oil brought permanent changes to the country.

From Dictators to Democracy

In 1908, before the oil boom changed the economic picture in Venezuela, another dictator had come to power. Juan Vicente Gómez was harsh, but few people dared oppose him because he often had them arrested and sometimes even killed. When oil began to bring money into Venezuela, Gómez used some of the new riches to build roads, railways, and ports. Instead of dealing directly with the foreign oil companies, Gómez gave control of the oil to his friends and relatives so that they could sell the drilling rights to foreigners. In this way, a small group of Venezuelans became very rich, while most stayed poor. This began to change only after Gómez died in 1935.

He was followed by two more generals, Eleazer López Contreras and Isaías Medina

Juan Vicente Gómez grew wealthy ruling Venezuela. He was said to be the richest person in South America.

Angarita. Both helped improve the country by spending more of the oil wealth to build hospitals and schools. Medina guided Venezuela through most of World War II. Although Venezuela didn't actively participate in the war, it provided much of the oil needed in the war.

By 1945, many Venezuelans were angry about a government system that didn't give them much freedom or access to wealth. A citizens' group joined with the military in 1945 to take over the government, but they were only successful until 1948. After another harsh dictatorship, the citizens' group returned to power in 1959. Rómulo Betancourt was the new president. Since then Venezuela has had a democratic government.

While Venezuela's rulers became rich, much of Venezuela lacked basic services. Here, Venezuelans transport water on donkeys.

In the 1970s, Venezuela's government took control of the iron, steel, and oil industries. By doing this, the country's leaders could control the money coming into the country. But the flow of money slowed down in 1983 when oil prices around the world took a sudden and deep drop. Venezuela's income fell quickly. The oil boom was over. Once again, Venezuelan citizens faced poverty and were unhappy with their government.

The Chávez Era

In 1992, a young military leader named Hugo Chávez led a coup attempt, trying to forcefully take over the government. His followers were angry with the unpopular president at the time, Carlos Andrés Pérez. Though his attempt was unsuccessful, Chávez was popular with the country's poor people. He, too, had been poor. Born in 1954 in the llanos, he is of mixed-race background. Chávez ran successfully for president in 1998, promising to bring greater freedom and wealth to average Venezuelans.

He quickly went to work, passing a new constitution in 1999, which gave the president more control. But these new powers were not enough to help him fix the economy and bring prosperity to the people. He was losing supporters fast.

In April 2002, a large opposition demonstration marched on the presidential palace, demanding that the president resign. Thousands of Chávez supporters were gathered there. Shots were fired, and more than twenty people died. The private media, which had called for the president's ouster, blamed the violence on the government. The military then took the president prisoner, demanding that he resign. The military installed a

Hugo Chávez won Venezuela's presidential election in 1998 with strong support from the poor and middle class.

new president, Pedro Carmona, but he did not remain in power. Intense pressure from Chávez supporters caused Carmona to resign just one day later. Chávez returned as president.

In December 2002, Chávez's opponents shut down the oil industry and other important parts of the economy in a second attempt to force out Chávez, but that failed, too. Finally, the opposition forced a recall election to determine whether to remove Chávez from office. In August 2004, Chávez won the election in a landslide, ending the long crisis.

In 2009 and 2010, Chávez and his supporters in government pushed through new reforms that granted more power for the president. These included laws that gave the federal government greater control over roads, ports, and airports, as well as many media outlets, banks, and the Internet. Many industries were placed under government ownership, and the opportunity for the National Assembly to debate new laws was limited. For eighteen months, Chávez was given the right to make laws by decree, meaning that the approval of the National Assembly was not required. The constitutional changes also ended term limits for elected officials in Venezuela. This allowed Chávez to be elected to another term as president in 2012.

Hugo Chávez remains controversial. In 2009, some people protested his new education law, which seemed to be inserting socialism into the curriculum.

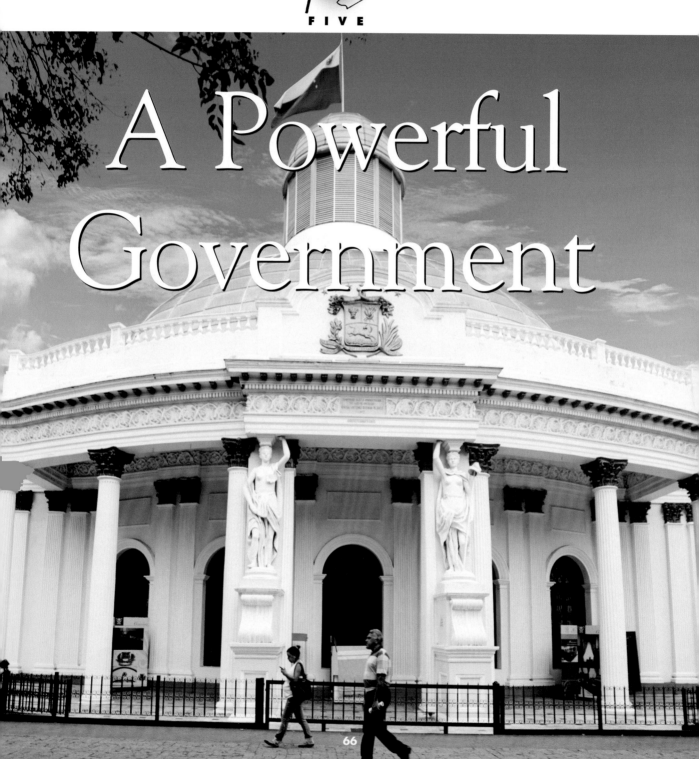

A Powerful Government

66

V ENEZUELA'S FULL NAME IS THE BOLIVARIAN Republic of Venezuela. It is a federal republic, which means that there is a division between the national, or federal, government and the local ones. The federal government has power over the military and economic policy, for example, while local governments control things such as roads and schools.

Venezuela has five branches of government, called powers. They are the executive, legislative, judicial, electoral, and citizen powers. Each has specific duties spelled out in the constitution. The most recent constitution was approved in 1999.

Opposite: **The National Assembly meets in the Federal Legislative Palace in Caracas.**

The Powers of Government

The executive power consists of the president, who is the head of government. He or she is elected to a six-year term. There are no limits on the number of terms an elected official can serve. The president chooses the vice president. The president also chooses how many people will be in the Council of Ministers, or cabinet, and appoints those ministers. Both the president and the vice president can suggest new laws and policies, but the National Assembly must approve those suggested laws and policies.

The Flag

Venezuela's flag has three broad horizontal stripes of yellow, blue, and red, with eight stars in a half-circle in the middle blue stripe. Sometimes the country's coat of arms appears in the upper-left corner within the yellow stripe. Venezuela's flag has had the same three colors since the nation became independent in 1811, but this exact design dates back only to 2006.

Yellow represents the wealth of the Venezuelan land. Red is for courage. And blue symbolizes independence from Spain. The stars represent Venezuela's provinces.

The legislative power consists of the National Assembly. It has 165 members who serve five-year terms. Their main role is to vote on legislation. They may propose new legislation as well.

The Supreme Tribunal of Justice heads the judicial power. It has six chambers, each judging different kinds of legal cases. Five of the chambers have five judges each, but the chamber that considers constitutional challenges has seven judges. The National Assembly elects the Supreme Tribunal judges to twelve-year terms. Venezuela also has lower courts, including district and municipal courts and courts of first instance. Trials in Venezuela are resolved during hearings before a judge and a jury.

The National Electoral Council heads the electoral power. The National Assembly elects its five members to seven-year terms. Several boards and commissions are also part of this power. They are supposed to make sure that elections on all levels are organized and legal.

The National Anthem

The lyrics to Venezuela's national anthem, *"Gloria al Bravo Pueblo"* ("Glory to the Brave People"), was written in 1810 by Vicente Salias. Juan José Landaeta later wrote the music. The song was adopted as the nation's anthem in 1885.

Spanish lyrics

> Gloria al bravo Pueblo
> que el yugo lanzó,
> la ley respetando la virtud y honor.
>
> ¡Abajo Cadenas! ¡Abajo Cadenas!
> gritaba el señor; gritaba el señor;
> y el pobre en su choza
> Libertad pidió:
> A este santo nombre tembló de pavor
> el vil egoísmo que otra vez triunfó.

English translation

> Glory to the brave nation
> Which shook off the yoke,
> Respecting law, virtue, and honor.
>
> "Off with the chains! Off with the chains!"
> Cried the Lord, cried the Lord,
> And the poor man in his hovel
> Implored freedom.
> At this holy name, there trembled
> The vile selfishness that had triumphed.

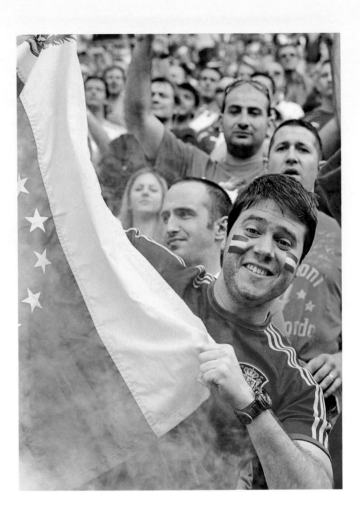

The Republican Moral Council makes up the citizen power. It includes a prosecutor general, a public defender, and the comptroller general. The National Assembly elects these officials to seven-year terms. Leadership of the group rotates among them. When they believe government actions violate the constitution or are illegal, they challenge them before the Supreme Tribunal of Justice. They try to make sure that public ethics and morals are upheld, and that public money is used properly.

State and Local Governments

State and local governments in Venezuela can make decisions without interference from the federal government in areas such as local roads and schools. The country is divided into twenty-three states, along with one federal district (the capital district

Members of the National Assembly must be at least twenty-one years old when they are elected. They can serve an unlimited number of terms.

Venezuela's National Government

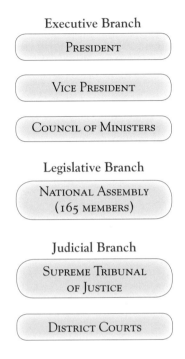

Executive Branch

President

Vice President

Council of Ministers

Legislative Branch

National Assembly
(165 members)

Judicial Branch

Supreme Tribunal
of Justice

District Courts

of Caracas) and one federal dependency. Voters from each state elect governors to four-year terms. Each state also has a legislative council with seven to fifteen members. The states are broken down further into districts, led by mayors and municipal councils.

The government is experimenting with a system of organizations called communal councils that are supposed to plan and carry out projects that local communities think are important. President Chávez believes this will put more control of the oil money in the hands of the people, but other Venezuelans believe that the councils are a way for him to weaken local governments and channel money to his supporters.

A Look at Caracas

Venezuela's capital city of Caracas is located in a beautiful valley at the base of Mount Ávila. It is named for the Caracas Indians, who inhabited the valley when it was founded in 1567. Within a decade, the city had become the capital of the Spanish Empire's Venezuela Province. One reason it grew to such importance was that the coastal mountains protected it from the pirate attacks that caused trouble in many other cities. In the 1680s, however, pirates managed to sneak in, ransack the city, and then set it ablaze.

When demand for chocolate grew around the world, cocoa production brought Caracas back to life, and the oil boom in the early to mid-1900s made the city an economic center of South America. Today, the city is home to about six million people.

Most of the city's economy is based on services, such as banking. Caracas is the headquarters for Venezuela's international oil dealings. The city also houses some industry, and produces chemicals, rubber, textiles, food, iron, cement, and leather.

Plaza Bolívar, at the heart of Caracas's old town, features a monument to Simón Bolívar (right, above) and is surrounded by lovely old architecture. The city contains many other parks and plazas as well. The *Teleférico*, a cable car, takes visitors to the top of Mount Ávila where they can enjoy stunning views of the city.

The city has many museums, including the Museum of Contemporary Art and the Museum of the Sciences. The theater at Teresa Carreño Cultural Complex is the second largest in South America. It puts on symphony and popular concerts, operas, ballets, and stage productions.

The vast differences between the lives of Venezuela's rich and poor are apparent in Caracas. Many huge mansions are in the city's wealthy east side. In the hills of the west side are barrios, poor neighborhoods where residents crowd together in flimsy houses, often without proper electricity and plumbing. All over Caracas, the streets are filled with cars. Pollution from auto exhaust often hangs in the air.

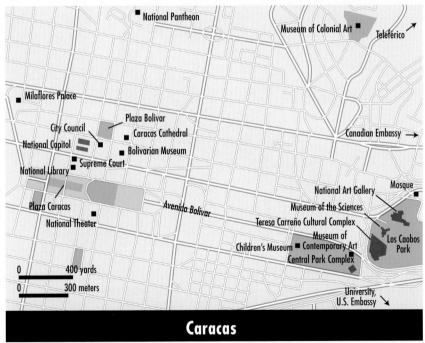

Caracas

An Oil Economy

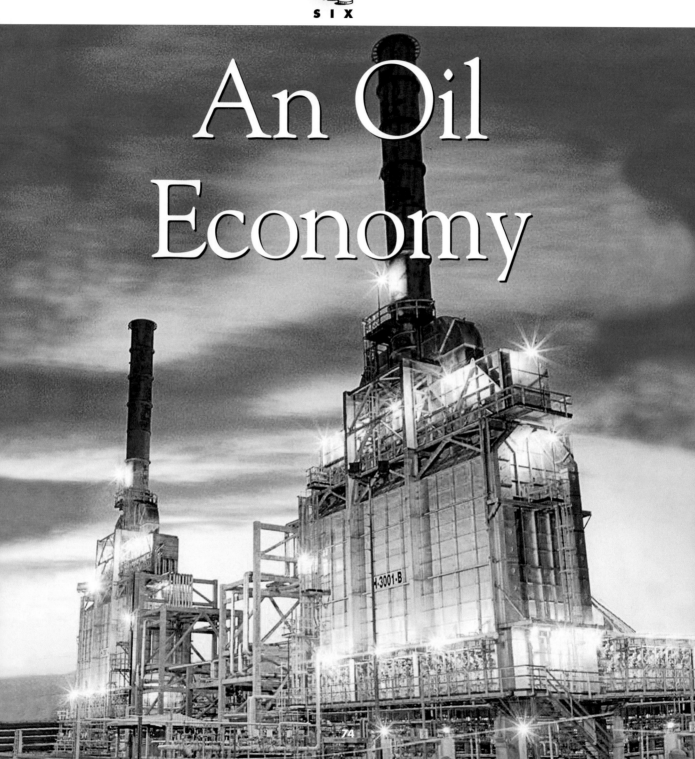

OIL HAS BEEN THE BACKBONE OF VENEZUELA'S economy since 1922. It produces nearly one-third of all the money Venezuela makes. That is both good and bad for the country.

It is good, because Venezuela was a very poor country before the oil boom brought in the money that turned the economy around. Even though the oil income per person in recent decades is not as great as it once was, Venezuela is still much better off than it would be without the oil.

The negative aspect of an oil-dependent economy is that the price of oil does not remain stable. Its value is often determined by shifting politics around the world. Venezuela faces a challenge each year trying to make economic decisions without knowing exactly how oil prices will impact the nation's finances.

Dependent on Oil

The danger of an economic system that was so dependent on oil hit Venezuela hard in 1983. For sixty years before, money

Opposite: **An oil refinery in José, Venezuela. Venezuela is the fifth-largest oil exporter in the world.**

Money Facts

Since 2008, the basic unit of currency in Venezuela has been the *bolívar fuerte*. It replaced the bolívar, which had been used since 1879. The bolívar had become worth very little, so the government replaced it. Venezuelans were allowed to exchange one thousand bolívares for every one bolívar fuerte. The word *fuerte* means "strong." It is a temporary addition to the name of the money to help distinguish it from the old currency. Eventually, the money will once again be called the bolívar. The bolívar fuerte is divided into one hundred céntimos. In 2012, $US1.00 was worth 4.3 bolívares fuertes.

Coins come in values of 1, 5, 10, 12.5, 25, and 50 céntimos, and 1 bolívar. Each features the value on one side, and the Venezuelan coat of arms on the other side. Bills have values of 2, 5, 10, 20, 50, and

100 bolívares. Each displays a hero from Venezuelan history on one side, and an endangered species on the other side. For example, Simón Bolívar is depicted on the front of the 100-bolívar bill, and the red siskin, an endangered bird, is on the back.

had flowed into the country. Venezuela built schools, roads, and hospitals. Thousands of jobs were created, and times were generally good. But 1983 brought a crash in oil prices around the world, and it took down Venezuela's economy along the way.

In 1976, the government took control of the oil industry and formed its own corporation, Petróleos de Venezuela, which gave the government strong influence over the economy. The nationalization of the oil companies meant that all profits now belonged to the government. People began to realize that politicians sometimes made business decisions that were beneficial to their personal situations rather than doing what was best for the nation as a whole.

Venezuelans realized just how dependent their country had been on oil. Little focus had been placed on any other industry. Nearly all the country's food came from outside of Venezuela. Manufacturing brought in very little money. In just a few years, Venezuela went from being South America's wealthiest nation to being one of its poorest. Most of the wealth remained in the hands of a small upper class, while many people had to live on very little.

A van stops to fill up at a gas station owned by the Petróleos de Venezuela (PDV), the state-owned oil company.

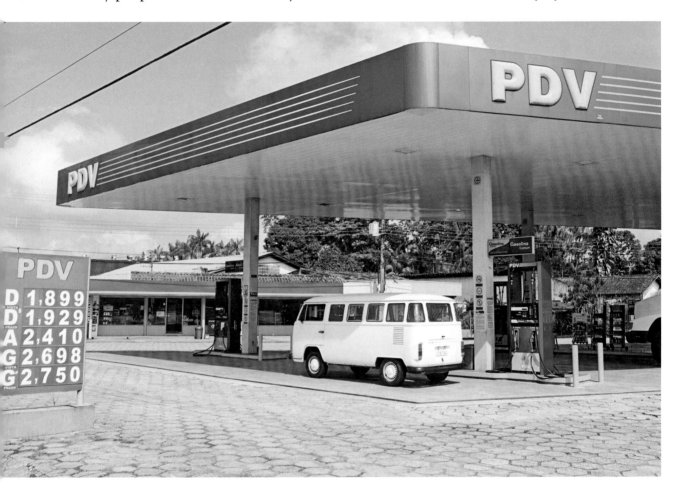

From the mid-1980s until the early 2000s, two-thirds of Venezuelans lived below the poverty line. Since then, Venezuela has been working to rebound. Most businesses and industries have been nationalized, or taken over by the government, just as the oil industry was. Today, the economy has improved to the point that only about one-third of the country's citizens are living in poverty. But Venezuelans continue to disagree about what direction the country should go in regarding government control of businesses.

Venezuela's energy minister serves as the president of the state-owned oil company. In 2012, Rafael Ramírez held the position.

The Oil Industry

Since the Venezuelan government controls the nation's oil through Petróleos de Venezuela, the government oil ministry decides how much oil is produced. This ministry also must approve agreements that Petróleos de Venezuela makes with other companies.

Venezuela has two main oil-producing regions. The first is Lake Maracaibo, where the nation's oil industry began. In recent years, even bigger deposits of oil have been found in the eastern part of Venezuela, in an area called the Orinoco Belt. It is now the largest oil-producing region in the country.

Oil wells in Lake Maracaibo. Because Venezuela has so much oil, the nation's gas prices are among the lowest of any country.

An Oil Economy **79**

A worker shovels baux-ite at a plant in southern Venezuela.

Oil production has fallen dramatically in recent years. In 2011, the country's oil wells produced 2.9 million barrels per day, compared to 3.5 million barrels each day in 1998. The government is slowing production on purpose, in an effort to keep prices higher. It is estimated that the country still has some 296.5 billion barrels in the ground. This is the most of any country in the world.

Oil sales to other countries make up about 95 percent of all the money Venezuela brings in from its exports. Nearly half of the money spent by the government comes from oil profits. Venezuela's most important trade partner is the United States, which purchases about half of all Venezuela's oil exports.

Mining

Riches beyond oil also lie underground in Venezuela. Major deposits of iron ore lie along the Orinoco River. It has been mined there since the 1940s. Other resources being mined include bauxite and phosphate rock. Bauxite is the raw material used to produce aluminum, while phosphate rock is used for such things as fertilizers and animal feed.

Gold and diamonds are also mined in Venezuela, in regions south of the Orinoco River. Right outside the Canaima National Park in the Gran Sabana region of Venezuela there

What Venezuela Grows, Makes, and Mines

Agriculture (2009)

Sugarcane	9,500,000 metric tons
Corn	2,800,000 metric tons
Rice	1,330,000 metric tons

Mining (2010)

Oil	985,000,000 barrels
Iron ore	15,200,000 metric tons
Bauxite	5,500,000 metric tons

Manufacturing (2004 value in bolívares fuertes)

Food products	8,100,000,000
Iron and steel	3,000,000,000
Refined petroleum products	2,900,000,000

Cacao beans must be dried before they can be ground and turned into chocolate.

is a huge crater—an open-pit mine—where some two hundred thousand miners are digging for diamonds and gold. They have no permits and pay no taxes to the government. Their gold and diamonds are sold to smugglers. The open pits cause major deforestation and pollution. International diamond dealers, environmentalists, and others have complained to the Venezuelan government, asking for an end to the illegal mining. Though the government has said it wants to stop the operation, little has been done to end it.

Manufacturing

Some of the nation's income from oil has been used to help build Venezuela's manufacturing industry. Manufacturing is once again growing in Venezuela. It employs about 10 percent of the labor force and provides about 15 percent of the nation's income. Petroleum products are among the chief items manufactured. Venezuelan factories also make iron and steel, processed foods, construction materials, textiles, aluminum, and motor vehicles.

Agriculture

Although 13 percent of Venezuela's labor force works in agriculture, it brings in less than 4 percent of the nation's income. About one-quarter of the country's land is used for agriculture. Corn, sugarcane, and rice are the main crops, but sorghum, bananas, cacao, vegetables, and coffee are also harvested. Animals are grown for beef and pork, as well as to provide milk and eggs. Special farms raise crab and shrimp.

Venezuela has rich farmland but does not produce enough food to feed its entire population. With so much money from oil, it is easy to import food instead. One of the main suppliers is the United States, which exports such agricultural products as wheat, soybeans, fruits, and dairy products.

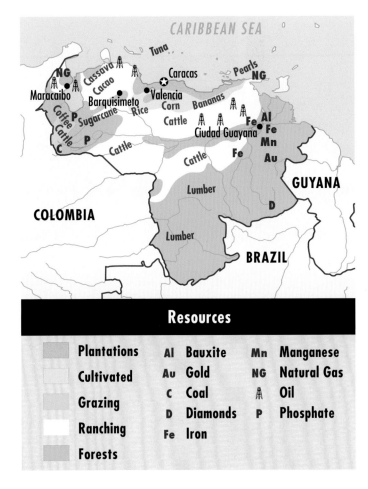

Resources

	Plantations	Al	Bauxite	Mn	Manganese
	Cultivated	Au	Gold	NG	Natural Gas
	Grazing	C	Coal	⚒	Oil
	Ranching	D	Diamonds	P	Phosphate
	Forests	Fe	Iron		

CHAPTER

SEVEN

People and Language

NEARLY SEVEN OUT OF TEN PEOPLE LIVING IN Venezuela are mestizo. This means they are of mixed race, with ethnicity that is some combination of native Indian, African, and European. Their backgrounds reflect the story of a nation once inhabited solely by native people, whose lives became interwoven with the Europeans who colonized their land and brought enslaved Africans there.

Opposite: **About 30 percent of Venezuelans are under age fifteen.**

A Blending of Backgrounds

When Europeans, mainly Spaniards, first arrived in Venezuela, they found small groups of people who lived successfully as hunters and gatherers. Some were nomadic, meaning that they moved from place to place to find the food they needed. Others were farmers, growing plants and raising animals.

As the colonists began to spread throughout Venezuela and other parts of South America, many indigenous Indians died. Many died from the diseases carried by the Europeans, while others died at the hands of cruel colonists who made them

Native people from along the Orinoco River pose for a photograph taken around 1900.

Ethnic Venezuela

Mestizo	69%
White	20%
Black	9%
Indigenous Indian	2%

slaves. Still more died when the Europeans forced them off their traditional lands into environments where they couldn't get the resources they needed to live. When the colonists first arrived, about forty or fifty different Indian groups lived in the land that is now Venezuela, but less than a century later, only about half remained.

The early colonists came as conquerors looking for gold. Most did not bring women with them on the long, difficult journey. They took native Indian women as brides, and their children became the first in Venezuela's large group of mestizos. As Spaniards colonized Venezuela, they began bringing in black slaves from Africa and the West Indies to work on plantations. These slaves, too, had mixed-raced children with the colonists.

Ethnic background was once an important factor in determining a person's social status in Venezuela. During colonial times and soon after, people who were more European were higher on the social ladder than people who were less European. But as more and more intermingling among the different ethnicities occurred through generations, this became less obvious and less important.

Today, 69 percent of the population is mestizo, while 20 percent is white. Venezuela continues to have a class structure that helps determine who holds power. Most of the country's wealthy and ruling elite are white, the descendants of European immigrants. Venezuela's poorest group is comprised mainly of people with African and indigenous Indian ancestry.

Miguel Cabrera made this painting of a Spanish man and his mestizo wife in the mid-1700s. Most people in Venezuela today are mestizo.

Venezuela today has twenty-eight indigenous, or native, groups. Four of these groups have more than ten thousand members. The largest is the Wayúu ethnic group that lives in the Guajira Peninsula along the Colombian border. The Wayúu people are also the most assimilated, meaning they've moved into cities and adapted to lives there. Many live in a poor suburb of Maracaibo, where the housing and schools are inadequate, and there is little clean water.

Guajiro women shop at a market in Zulia Province, near the Colombian border.

The least assimilated group is the Yanomami people. The fifteen thousand Yanomami people remain quite isolated, living along tributaries of the Amazon and Orinoco Rivers in southern Venezuela. The government has vowed to help them preserve their territory, but outsiders, particularly gold miners, continue to exploit their land. Some Yanomami have been killed in skirmishes with the miners, and more have died from the diseases introduced by the miners.

Yanomami women pierce their noses and lips and thread sticks through the holes. Both men and women use body paint on special occasions.

Pedestrians cross a busy intersection in Caracas. Most Venezuelans live in cities.

Persons per square mile		Persons per square kilometer
more than 260		more than 100
131–260		51–100
26–130		11–50
3–25		1–10
fewer than 3		fewer than 1

Indian communities are fighting to hang on to their cultures, but they face many threats. Illegal mining and ever-expanding cattle ranching operations are moving into their territories. Christian missionaries are challenging their native religions. Many indigenous people are choosing to leave their traditional communities, heading to cities in the hopes of obtaining more money.

But in the city life can be just as hard, and sometimes worse. Some employers refuse to hire indigenous people, so the Indians are forced to provide for their families any way they can. In Ciudad Guayana, many Indians spend the day picking through the garbage at a city dump, looking for metal, clothing, or any item they could sell. Often, the adults are joined by their children, who pick through the rubble instead of going to school. This is dangerous work, and exposes people to diseases such as malaria and tuberculosis, which spread quickly.

An Urban Nation

Venezuela is a very urban country. About 88 percent of its twenty-nine million people live in large cities and their surrounding suburbs. It is one of the most urbanized nations in all of Latin America. All of the major cities, including Caracas, Maracaibo, Valencia, and Barquisimeto, are located in the northern part of the country, mostly along the coast. Though just about half of Venezuela's land lies south of the Orinoco River, only 5 percent of the population lives there.

Venezuela is also a very young country. Children under age fifteen make up about 30 percent of the population, while those over sixty-five are roughly 5 percent. In the United States, by comparison, 20 percent of the population is under fifteen, and 13 percent is over sixty-five.

Venezuela's Largest Cities (2012 est.)	
Caracas	6,000,000
Maracaibo	1,891,800
Valencia	1,408,400
Barquisimeto	1,018,900
Ciudad Guayana	789,500

Venezuela's Indigenous University

The Venezuelan Indigenous University is one of the world's most unusual schools. It offers classes in raising buffalo; ancient cultures; and land rights law. The university was founded in the early twenty-first century in Tauca, amid the forests of southern Venezuela. The university was established to teach young people the skills they need to be successful community leaders, and help safeguard the land, rights, and ancient cultures of their communities. Although fewer than one hundred students attend the school, each indigenous community nationwide sends at least one young person. Students live on campus, sleeping in hammocks and cooking on open fires. Though the government helps to fund the university, organizers are trying to provide more funding on their own, so the school will be free of government control. They see their school as a model and would like to see similar universities set up for indigenous peoples throughout South America.

Language

Venezuela has many official languages. The most common is Spanish, but the government recognizes about thirty languages spoken by the country's indigenous Indians. These fall into three main catagories: Arawakan, Cariban, and Chibchan. These native languages are dying out, however, as increasing numbers of indigenous people move to cities in search of more comfortable, modern lives. Some languages are spoken by only a small number of people. Anthropologists, people who study cultures, are trying to quickly learn these languages and document them before they are lost forever.

Many Venezuelans who attend universities are learning to speak English as a second language. They know it will help them communicate in business and scientific areas with people from many parts of the world. Other common languages in Venezuela include Portuguese, Chinese, Italian, Arabic, and French.

In tourist areas, signs are sometimes written in both Spanish and English.

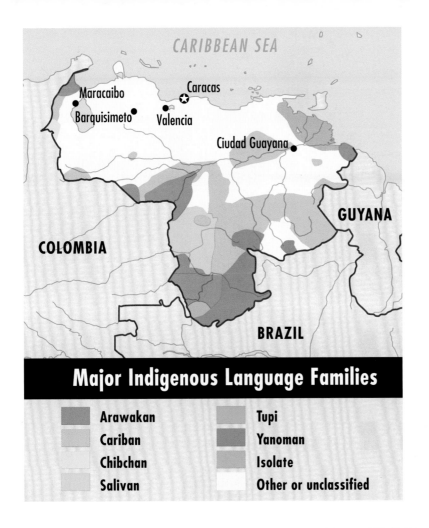

Major Indigenous Language Families

- Arawakan
- Cariban
- Chibchan
- Salivan
- Tupi
- Yanoman
- Isolate
- Other or unclassified

Common Spanish Phrases

Buenos días	Good morning
Buenas noches	Good evening
Hola, me llamo . . .	Hello, my name is . . .
Mucho gusto.	Nice to meet you.
Por favor	Please
Gracias	Thank you
De nada	You're welcome
Lo siento.	I'm sorry.
Hasta luego.	See you later.
Adiós	Good-bye

Religious Life

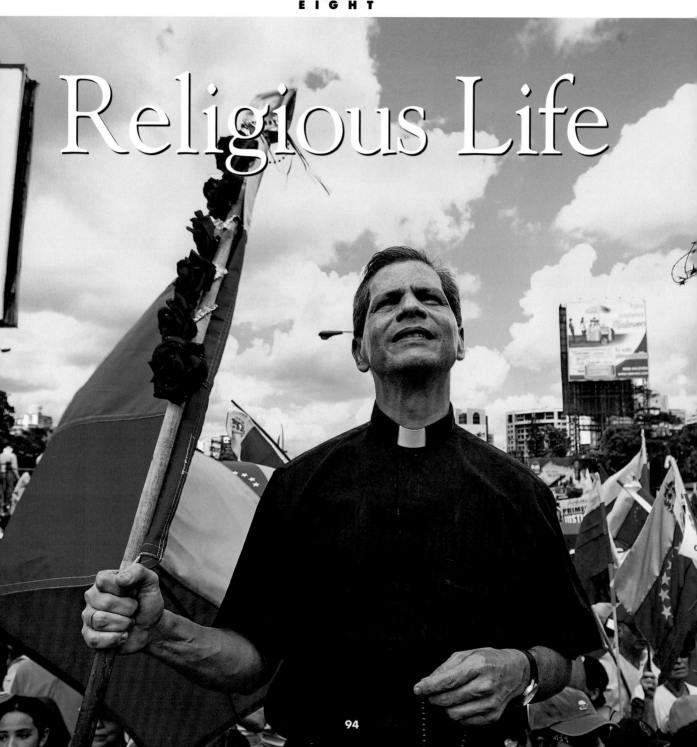

ALTHOUGH THERE IS NO OFFICIAL RELIGION OF Venezuela, there is a dominant one. More than 90 percent of all Venezuelans consider themselves Roman Catholics. Only a few, mostly in the middle class, go to mass regularly. Many also hold beliefs that come from ancestors who were Indians or enslaved Africans. Today, many poor Venezuelans in the cities go to Protestant churches.

Opposite: **A priest attends a political rally in Caracas.**

Venezuela's Catholic History

Catholic missionaries have been in Venezuela since the early 1500s. They arrived in northeastern Venezuela in 1515. Their attempt at converting the indigenous peoples to Catholicism failed, however. Since the local people had been treated terribly by early explorers who had ransacked their villages, they wanted revenge, so they killed the missionaries.

Missionaries arrived in Venezuela in the early 1500s, but they had little success in converting the indigenous peoples.

It was not until 1650 that missionaries were actually successful. In the land that is now the northern state of Anzoátegui, missionaries set up communities called *pueblos de indios*, or Indian towns, near the homes of the Píritu Indians. The missionaries sometimes used gifts to attract the Indians to these settlements. Other times they just captured the Indians and forced them to live there. Once they were in the settlements, the Indians were forced to listen over and over to lectures about the wrongs of their native religions and the sins they were committing against Christianity. Eventually, most Indians in the pueblos de indios became Christians. They provided labor for the town and were allowed to keep half their profits, while the other half went to supporting the missionaries and the king of Spain.

Since conversions were successful in these settlements, more missionaries arrived to set up more pueblos de indios. They were established throughout Venezuela, with a large number near Caracas. These communities brought some organization to Venezuelan society and helped join the nation together. But the native population paid a great price. Much of their culture was lost. Their native religions were destroyed. It is because of these communities that Venezuela is a mostly Catholic nation today.

Construction of the Caracas Cathedral began in 1666. The church has been expanded and changed many times.

The Catholic religion was firmly established as a part of Venezuelan life by the early 1800s. Caracas was the center of Catholic leadership in the nation. In cities, small towns, and villages throughout Venezuela, the church was the center of society.

But the church's status in Venezuela eventually changed. In the nineteenth century, strong-willed political parties with determined leadership took control of the country. They saw

The Roman Catholic Church

The Roman Catholic Church has more than one billion followers worldwide, making it the largest single Christian faith. Neighborhood parishes, usually led by a priest, are at the base of the church structure. These are organized into regional dioceses, which are led by bishops. The major church in each diocese is called a cathedral. Several dioceses combine in large groups to form archdioceses, led by archbishops. At the head of the church is the pope, who is also the leader of Vatican City in Rome, Italy, the home of the Catholic Church.

Catholics, like all Christians, believe that God came to earth in the form of his son, Jesus. The life and teachings of Jesus, found in the New Testament of the Bible, form the basis of Catholic beliefs. Unlike other Christians, Catholics also venerate, or worship, saints. They believe that when they pray to saints their prayers are taken directly to God. The feast days of saints are celebrated throughout the year. These feast days are important in Venezuela, where cities and villages often stage colorful festivals on the feast days of their patron saints.

how devoted people were to the church and wanted citizens to be devoted to their political party instead. They changed laws to weaken the Catholic Church. For example, laws forced cemeteries to remove religious symbols. Seminaries, where priests trained, were forced to shut down. The government took over property that belonged to Catholic organizations. It banned religious ceremonies that once accompanied special events, such as weddings and funerals. Government leaders tried to eliminate religion from the ceremonies.

Today, crosses are common in Venezuelan cemeteries, but for a time in the nineteenth century, they were not allowed.

Religious Holidays

Christian holidays are widely celebrated in Venezuela. Easter and Christmas are the major religious events, but minor holidays are also celebrated. The festivities are not solely religious. There are parades and carnivals featuring lots of dancing, music, and good food. Most communities and parishes have specific patron saints they honor with parties on their feast days. Here are the major religious holidays in Venezuela:

Epiphany	January 6
Holy Thursday	Spring
Good Friday	Spring
Easter	Spring
Ascension	Late Spring
Corpus Christi	Early Summer
Assumption	August 15
All Saints' Day	November 1
Immaculate Conception	December 8
Christmas	December 25

In 1820, there were 640 Catholic priests in Venezuela. By 1855, only 154 priests remained. More than half the churches sat empty. In 1870, Antonio Guzmán Blanco became president of Venezuela. He worked hard to eliminate the Catholic Church in Venezuela. He forced the church leadership out of

Caracas and ended all ties with the Vatican, the headquarters of the Catholic Church in Rome, Italy. By this time, the church appeared to have little presence at all left in Venezuela.

This did not mean, however, that people stopped being Catholic. Instead, they hid their faith from view. Since formal church practices had been banned, families conducted informal religious practices instead. The Catholic faith was passed down from generation to generation, frequently by mothers and grandmothers. Priests, churches, and other aspects of the official Catholic Church became less important. This more personalized form of Catholicism took hold in Venezuela, and it remains a common practice in modern times.

Venezuelans attend a mass in Caracas.

Religion in Venezuela

Roman Catholic	96%
Protestant	2%
Other	2%

Religion Today

The Catholic Church regained some of its influence in Venezuela beginning in the early 1900s. In particular, many Catholic schools were established and staffed by priests and other religious leaders. Today, the schools continue to operate. Many of them have the specific mission to educate Venezuela's poorest children. While the number of Catholics remains high, far fewer—less than 20 percent of the population—regularly attend church services.

Protestant religions have attracted more followers during the past few decades. A number of Protestant missionaries work among the poor and have brought people into their faiths. A small percentage of Jewish people live in Venezuela, mostly in Caracas and Maracaibo, as do a few Muslims, followers of Islam.

The Good Doctor

The Roman Catholic Church does not officially consider José Gregorio Hernández a saint, but that does not stop many Venezuelans from viewing him as their most beloved and important saint. His image is displayed in homes and shrines around the country. He is usually depicted dressed in a suit, with a felt hat and small mustache.

Hernández was born in 1864 in the Andes Mountains. He studied medicine in Caracas and became an important doctor. Although he tended to the president of Venezuela, he preferred to serve the country's poor citizens for free. He was very religious and tried to live quietly in a monastery for a time, but he soon returned to taking care of Venezuela's neediest people.

After Hernández died in a car accident in 1919, many people began giving him credit for miracles. Soon, he had a huge following that continues today.

Mixing Faiths

Not many people follow the religions once practiced by Venezuela's indigenous peoples. Missionaries wiped out these religions in their quest to convert the native people to Catholicism. Still, there are some religious beliefs that were founded in Venezuela long ago that continue to attract many followers today. Sometimes these religions are called cults. Most often, people follow the cults in addition to the Catholic faith, creating a blend of religious practices unique to Venezuela. The most popular of these by far is the Cult of María Lionza.

A barefoot man dances over burning wood during a ceremony that is part of the Cult of María Lionza.

A statue of María Lionza riding a tapir overlooks a highway in Caracas.

The Cult of María Lionza is based near the small town of Chivacoa, just east of Barquisimeto in the Andes, but has spread throughout Venezuela. It is estimated that between 10 and 30 percent of Venezuelans are followers. They represent all layers of Venezuelan society, from poor farmers in small rural villages to wealthy government leaders in Caracas.

The cult honors many gods, spirits, and other beings, including Simón Bolívar. The most important figure is María Lionza herself. The story of her life and how the religion was founded have been passed down through many generations. Over the years, so many different versions of the story have emerged that no one is certain whether she was a real human being or not. Some say she was born in 1502, the daughter of an indigenous leader in Yaracuy state, in northwestern Venezuela. Today, she is often referred to as *La Reina*, the Queen. She is depicted as a powerful woman riding on a tapir and is revered as a goddess of nature and harmony.

Some people claim to be able to act on her behalf. They are said to be able to heal the sick, tell the future, and communicate with the dead. The cult's rituals include rhythmic music and dance, which causes some people to fall into a trance. The main place of worship for the cult is a mountainside near Chivacoa. The site is filled with outdoor altars and shrines. On October 12, the cult's most important holiday, tens of thousands of people show up at the site to take part in ceremonies.

People in the Cult of María Lionza attend a ceremony to promote good health. The religion blends Catholicism with traditional indigenous and African beliefs.

A Spirited Culture

THE VENEZUELAN PEOPLE EMBRACE LIFE WITH GUSTO. They enjoy good music, lively dance, great beauty, and competitive sports.

Music

The most popular and traditional Venezuelan music is *joropo*. This fast-paced music is performed throughout the country. The leading instrument in the joropo is *arpa llanera,* or plains harp. Sometimes a performer will sing, accompanied by maracas and a small guitar, called a *cuatro.*

Gaita is another popular type of music to come out of Venezuela. Its roots are in the Maracaibo region. Gaita is a lively music, based on drumbeats and vocals. It is usually performed by small groups, which include at least one guitar and a couple of drums. Lyrics are often improvised on the spot and frequently refer to politics or religion. Gaita is particularly popular during the Christmas season, when it is performed in many places, including in buses, restaurants, and on the beach.

Gustavo Dudamel is a rising star in the world of classical music. At age twenty-eight, he became the director of the Los Angeles Philharmonic in California.

Simón Díaz, a Venezuelan folksinger, is one of the country's most beloved entertainers. Born in 1928, he began his musical career performing the traditional music of the llanos region. He has since performed around the world and recorded more than seventy albums. He has also been a television actor, a poet, and a writer. In 2008 he received a Lifetime Achievement Award from the Latin Grammys.

Classical music is also extremely popular in Venezuela. The country is known for its strong music education program. More than three hundred thousand children, most from poor backgrounds, attend publicly funded music schools around the country. The government supports 125 youth orchestras. The best students from these orchestras go on to play in the Simón Bolívar Symphony Orchestra.

Gustavo Dudamel has been the artistic director of the Simón Bolívar Symphony Orchestra since 1999. Dudamel, himself a product of Venezuela's music education program, is one of the world's leading conductors. He is the principal conductor of the Gothenburg Symphony in Sweden and the music director of the Los Angeles Philharmonic in California.

Most young Venezuelans also listen to modern popular music and many of the singers and bands that are enjoyed around the world. Some Venezuelan groups have gained widespread popularity. Los Amigos Invisibles earned worldwide fame for their lively mix of funk, disco, jazz, and Latin rhythms. They began playing together in Caracas in 1991 and are still turning out award-winning music today.

Los Amigos Invisibles won a Latin Grammy for their album *Commercial* in 2009.

Dance

Joropo music has a traditional dance that accompanies it, also known as joropo. Partners perform this folk dance, which has influences from both Africa and Europe. The dance uses the whole body. Dancers turn their hands, and take quick, small steps at first. Gradually, the couple joins arms and the woman makes large, sweeping steps while the man stomps to the rhythm of the music.

Professional dancing is also found in Venezuela, where there are several fine ballet companies, as well as companies performing contemporary dance.

The Dancing Devils

On the Feast of Corpus Christi, a solemn Catholic holiday and one of the holiest days of the year, people masquerade as devils and dance in the streets of Venezuela. But nowhere is the festival celebrated with more enthusiasm than in San Francisco de Yare in Miranda state in the northern part of the country. Each year during the festival, crowds of people dress in red costumes topped with huge and hideous devil masks. Then they make their way through town, marching, leaping, and swaying to the rhythm of the drums that accompany them.

At the end of the procession, the dancing "devils" go to church, completing this ceremony that celebrates the victory of good in its struggle with evil. Some Venezuelans believe this ceremony helps protect them against disasters and brings them good crops and health.

The devil dances display both the Spanish and the African roots of Venezuelans. The images of the devil come from Spanish religious tales, while the rhythmic drumbeats and dancing are a part of African culture. The result is a festive celebration that is uniquely Venezuelan.

Venezuelan women won the Miss Universe title in 2008 and 2009. Never before had contestants from the same country won two years in a row.

Beauty Pageants

Beauty pageants are hugely popular in Venezuela. In the past three decades, more women crowned Miss Venezuela have gone on to win international titles than representatives from any other country. These include six Miss Universe, six Miss World, and six Miss International crowns.

Pageants are big business in Venezuela. Caracas is the site of an expensive school, the Miss Venezuela Academy, where young women learn pageant secrets. They are trained in onstage poise and taught how to enhance their beauty and perform in an interview. The training goes on for months. It is also a great honor for fashion designers to create the gowns worn by contestants.

Irene Sáez won the Miss Universe title before entering politics.

Winning the title of Miss Venezuela typically assures the young woman of success in a career as an actress, television personality, or model. Some winners have gone on to other professions. Most notably, Irene Sáez, who was crowned Miss Universe in 1981, became the mayor of Caracas, a governor, and in 1998 a Venezuelan presidential candidate.

Some Venezuelans criticize the pageants and the importance placed on them. They feel that too much emphasis is put on a type of beauty that few people can achieve, and that more effort should be spent on developing intelligence instead. Others see Venezuela's beauty pageant success as a source of great national pride.

Sports

Baseball is the most popular sport in Venezuela by far. Baseball likely arrived in Venezuela with Americans who came to the country to work during the early days of the oil boom. After the Venezuelan Professional Baseball League was formed in 1945, the country was hooked. Today, the league includes eight teams. Many Venezuelans also follow North American baseball. They particularly enjoy watching Venezuelan players who have made it to *Las Grandes Ligas*, "the Big Leagues."

The National Art Gallery

Venezuela's *Galería de Arte Nacional,* the National Art Gallery in Caracas, is dedicated to the preservation of Venezuelan art. Its permanent collection holds seven thousand pieces, representing nearly five centuries of Venezuelan art. Works range from ancient pre-Hispanic sculptures to modern plastic pieces that move. Perhaps the most important work on display is an 1896 painting, *Miranda en La Carraca,* by Arturo Michelena, which depicts the revolutionary leader Francisco de Miranda in a Spanish jail, awaiting his death.

Nearly three hundred Venezuelan baseball players have gone on to professional careers with U.S. and Canadian major league teams. The first was Alex Carrasquel, who pitched for the Washington Senators from 1939 to 1945. Luis Aparicio, a shortstop with the Chicago White Sox from 1956 to 1962 and then again from 1968 to 1970, is in the Baseball Hall of Fame. Ozzie Guillen has had great success, first as a shortstop and then

Boys stretch during a training session at a baseball school in Caracas.

as a manager. Elvis Andrus, who was born in Maracay in 1988, was the second-youngest player in the American League when he joined the Texas Rangers in 2009 at the age of twenty.

Other Sports

Many Venezuelans are fans of soccer, which is called football in most of the world. People all around the country cheer on the Venezuelan National Football Team. The team's deep red shirts have given them the nickname *La Vinotinto*, "the Burgundy." Until recent years, the team had not been very successful, in part because many young Venezuelans with athletic talent played baseball instead. But soccer's status has been growing, and so has the success of the team.

Ozzie Guillen

Many Venezuelans have played Major League baseball in the United States, but few have been as successful as Oswaldo "Ozzie" Guillen. He was born in Ocumare del Tuy, in northern Venezuela, in 1964. He began his Major League career playing shortstop for the Chicago White Sox in 1985, and he was named the American League Rookie of the Year. During Guillen's long career, he was recognized for both his outstanding skill and his exuberant love of the game. In 2004, he became manager of the Chicago White Sox, and the following year he led the team to its first World Series win since 1917. He is the first Latino manager in Major League history to lead a team to a World Series championship. He was the manager of the Miami Marlins for the 2012 season.

Many Venezuelans think bullfighting should be banned because the bulls are injured and usually killed.

While soccer is growing in popularity, another sport is losing fans. Spaniards brought the practice of bullfighting to Venezuela when they first arrived there hundreds of years ago. A traditional Venezuelan form of bullfighting is *toros coleados*, in which the bullfighter grabs the bull by the tail and throws the animal down. Bullfighting was once a beloved sport in Venezuela, but it has come under fire in recent years as people have become more sensitive to animal cruelty. Fewer and fewer people attend the fights, and some cities have stopped them entirely. Some people have attempted to pass national laws to ban bullfighting, but this has not been successful.

Other spectator sports growing in popularity include horse racing, basketball, rugby, cycling, and golf. But Venezuelan people enjoy participating in sports, too. Some like the heart-pounding thrill of white-water rafting or kayaking on the Orinoco, while others try their luck at sport fishing off the coast. Hiking is also popular in many parts of Venezuela's beautiful countryside.

Daily Life

I F SOMEONE FROM A BIG CITY IN THE UNITED STATES or Canada were suddenly transported to a busy center of a Venezuelan city, it might seem very familiar. People have the same range of appearance in Venezuela as they do in North America. Fashions are similar, and so are the architecture, traffic, and often the music. Some aspects of life in this South American country, however, are uniquely Venezuelan.

Opposite: **Fruit is an important part of the Venezuelan diet.**

Food

Venezuelans typically eat a wide variety of food. Beef and seafood are popular. Fresh fruits and vegetables are readily available, including oranges, papayas, passion fruit, limes, avocados, strawberries, pineapples, watermelon, tomatoes, onions, cucumbers, beans, and lettuce.

Many Venezuelans begin the day with a hearty breakfast. It often includes eggs and some vegetables accompanied by milk, fruit juice, or hot chocolate, and strong coffee. Lunch is usually the largest meal of the day, in part because many

Arepas can be filled with all types of foods. This one contains avocado, cheese, and ham.

Venezuelans have two hours or more off from work in the middle of the day. They return home to escape the midday heat, enjoy meals with their families, and rest. Most have a light dinner in the evening.

During at least one meal every day, Venezuelans will probably eat *arepas*. They are a staple of Venezuelan cuisine. Arepas are thick cornmeal pancakes that are filled or topped with other foods. Fried eggs, seafood, and seasoned meats are common fillings. So are cheeses, jelly, and vegetables such as onions and tomatoes. Some people stuff arepas with more unusual fare, such as shark, octopus, or quail eggs. Sauces add even more variety and flavor to this dish. People sometimes add avocado mixtures such as guacamole, or maybe a spicy hot sauce.

Pabellón Criollo

Pabellón criollo is a common traditional meal in Venezuela that many people consider the national dish. Have an adult help you with this recipe.

Ingredients

2 pounds beef sirloin

¼ cup oil

2 onions, chopped

2 teaspoons salt

1 teaspoon pepper

4 cloves garlic, minced

1 red bell pepper, chopped

Cumin (optional)

3 cups tomatoes, peeled, seeded, and chopped

Directions

To prepare pabellón criollo, cook the beef sirloin in the oil for about 5 minutes on each side. Then place the meat in a large pot, along with one chopped onion, salt, and pepper. Add enough water to cover it all. Simmer it over low heat for about one hour, or until the meat is very tender.

Remove the meat from the mixture and let it cool. Save the broth. When the meat is cool, shred it with your fingers or with two forks. Then, sauté the other chopped onion in a pan, along with the minced garlic and the red pepper. Use a little oil if necessary, and add salt and pepper to taste. Cumin seed may also be added. When the vegetables are soft, stir in the meat and tomatoes. Add enough of the remaining broth to moisten the mixture, and simmer it over low heat for about 15 minutes.

Serve the meat along with rice, beans, and plantains. Enjoy!

Another common meal is pabellón criollo, a dish of seasoned pulled beef served with rice and beans. Though this combination is popular throughout much of Latin America, the seasonings make this dish special to Venezuela. It is often served along with fried plantains, which are similar to North American bananas but are firmer and less sweet. The dish is sometimes topped with a fried egg. Fish, caiman, or capybara meat may be substituted for the beef.

In Venezuela, few meals are complete without dessert. Favorites include carrot cake and coconut cake. Churros, fried dough sprinkled with cinnamon and sugar, are another popular dessert.

Education

In Venezuela, children must go to school once they turn six years old, but many also attend preschool when they are younger. Children attend primary school from ages six to eleven. Secondary education lasts until age fifteen. When stu-

Hallacas

To Venezuelans, the *hallaca*, a type of meat pie, is a food that means Christmas! Hallacas are typically made with a mixture of beef, pork, and chicken, as well as capers, raisins, and olives. This filling is wrapped twice, first in cornmeal dough and then in plantain leaves. The hallacas are then either steamed or boiled. Preparing hallacas takes a lot of work, and the whole family usually helps out. Together, they are making good food and good memories.

dents reach ninth grade, they choose to focus either on science and math or on humanities, such as literature, music, and art. They follow their chosen educational path for the next two years. This choice affects a student's college program and eventual career. It can be a lot of pressure for a young person.

In many cities, students go to school in shifts. Some students attend classes from early morning to early afternoon, while others are in school from mid-afternoon until early evening. This saves money because twice as many students use one school building.

All students in Venezuela wear uniforms, with different grade levels wearing different colored shirts. Grades seven through nine wear blue shirts.

Playing Games

Many children who belong to Venezuela's indigenous groups live quite differently from other young people in Venezuela. Some indigenous communities are isolated, so the children do not have outside influences that determine what they eat and wear. Even the games the children play are different.

Indigenous children often play with items that are small versions of things adults use. Boys often play with toy canoes and toy bows and arrows. Dolls made of wood, clay, or shells are common for girls. These toys help the children learn about the tasks they will perform as they grow older.

All children by law must go to school, but some poor children do not because they are working to help their families. The nation's literacy rate, the percentage of adults who can read, is about 95 percent.

Body Language

Venezuelans tend to be expressive and outgoing. When they meet, women often greet people with whom they're familiar with a kiss on each cheek, while two men meeting will clasp hands with a hearty grip and a shake. Venezuelans stand close to one another, sometimes touching while talking, as a way of showing care and concern. They often motion with their hands as they talk, sometimes so wildly that a friendly conversation may appear to be an argument.

Some gestures have very different meanings in Venezuela than they do in other cultures. For example, in the United States people sometimes put their thumb and forefinger together in a circle to mean "OK." But this gesture is an insult in Venezuela. It is also rude to point at someone. In Venezuela, it is preferred to simply gesture in someone's direction with the entire hand.

Almost nine hundred thousand students attend the nation's ninety-plus universities each year. About 70 percent of them are from the wealthiest segment—about 20 percent—of the country. The government has been working to get more children from less wealthy families into the nation's universities.

Clothing

Throughout Venezuela, the fashions worn are much like those seen in the warmer climates of the United States. In Venezuela, people take a lot of pride in looking good, and most put an effort into their appearance. Whether rich or poor, they typically try to wear clothes that are neat and attractive. Jeans and T-shirts are popular with younger people. Professional women wear blouses and skirts, dresses, and business suits, and men wear dark business suits.

Venezuelans at a café on Margarita Island. Most Venezuelans wear the same kinds of clothes as people do in the United States.

Carolina Herrera, Fashion Designer

Carolina Herrera, the daughter of a former governor of Caracas, is one of the world's most respected fashion designers. Born in 1939 in Caracas, she founded her own company in 1980. It is now based in New York City. Herrera's designs often feature deep, bright colors and intricate patterns. Many prominent women have worn her clothes, including the former U.S. first lady Jacqueline Kennedy Onassis. Herrera has received many awards during her long career, including Womenswear Designer of the Year in 2004.

Traditional Venezuelan clothes for women included colorful, full-skirted dresses. The traditional outfit for men was a white suit with a rounded collar. Few people wear these today. They are only worn as costumes for folk dances and other events.

National Holidays

New Year's Day	January 1
Holy Thursday	Spring
Good Friday	Spring
Declaration of Independence	April 19
Labor Day	May 1
Battle of Carabobo	June 24
Independence Day	July 5
Birth of Simón Bolívar	July 24
Civil Servants' Day	September 4
Day of Indigenous Resistance	October 12
Christmas Day	December 25

A Child Is Born

Most Venezuelans celebrate births in much the same way as people do in North America. It is a joyous occasion, and families gather to welcome the newborn into the family. People traditionally bring gifts. Most Venezuelans are baptized as babies, as is the tradition among Roman Catholics.

Venezuela's indigenous Indians have a variety of birth customs. Nearly all have taboos against mothers, and sometimes fathers, eating certain types of meat and fish during the pregnancy. It is believed that eating these foods can negatively affect the baby's health.

Housing

Nothing in Venezuelan life showcases the difference between rich and poor more than housing does. Many wealthy Venezuelans live in luxurious homes in secure gated communities on the outskirts of cities. Middle-class people typically live in high-rise apartment buildings in cities. Many poor Venezuelans live in *ranchos*, houses they built themselves in poorer neighborhoods, called barrios. Over time, some Venezuelans turn their ranchos into nice homes in which they take great pride. But in many barrios, the houses are made of corrugated steel, clay, or cement. Some have dirt floors with only one room. Many barrios are built on the hillsides outside large cities, right next to garbage dumps and filthy industrial sites. The houses sometimes slide down the hillsides during heavy rains.

In 2010 and 2011, Venezuela experienced serious flooding. More than 130,000 people were left homeless. Many of them moved to the nation's capital of Caracas, a city that already had a large homeless population. People were living in abandoned warehouses and shopping malls.

In response, the government began what is called the Great Housing Mission. This program is designed to build two hundred thousand homes at a cost of US$16 billion. Although it is providing housing for people in need, the program is sometimes controversial. Many of the homes are being built in the center of Caracas, an area that is already crowded. The government forced some landowners to give up their property so new apartment buildings could be built there. Landowners were told they would be paid fairly for their property, but many say that they did not receive the money.

Brightly colored houses are stacked on a hillside in a poor suburb of Caracas.

Life is also difficult for those people moving into the new high-rise buildings. Many people receiving housing under the program were used to life in small communities. In those towns and villages, many had earned a living fishing or selling handicrafts, vegetables, or baked goods from their homes. That kind of lifestyle is not possible in high-rise apartments in the middle of Caracas. The people have to find new ways to make a living.

Caracas is full of tall apartment buildings.

New Ways

The people of Venezuela have a long history of learning new ways to get by. After centuries of Spanish rule, they learned quickly how to fight for their freedom and govern their own country. Venezuela was a poor country that rapidly became wealthy with the oil boom and then, just as quickly, became a poor nation once again. Through it all, its people have adapted and survived. Through dictatorships and democracies, through wealth and poverty, Venezuelans have carried on with pride. They remain resilient, prepared to meet the next challenge.

Timeline

Venezuelan History

First people arrive in what is now Venezuela. **14,000** BCE

People in Venezuela make clay bowls and jugs. **1000** BCE

Christopher Columbus leads the first European voyage to Venezuela. **1498** CE

Italian explorer Amerigo Vespucci names the region Venezuela. **1499**

Cumaná becomes the first Spanish town in continental South America. **1521**

Caracas is founded. **1567**

Venezuela becomes the first Spanish colony to declare its independence. **1811**

Simón Bolívar is elected president of the Republic of Gran Colombia, as Venezuela is known at this time. **1819**

World History

ca. 2500 BCE The Egyptians build the pyramids and the Sphinx in Giza.

ca. 563 BCE The Buddha is born in India.

313 CE The Roman emperor Constantine legalizes Christianity.

610 The Prophet Muhammad begins preaching a new religion called Islam.

1054 The Eastern (Orthodox) and Western (Roman Catholic) Churches break apart.

1095 The Crusades begin.

1215 King John seals the Magna Carta.

1300s The Renaissance begins in Italy.

1347 The plague sweeps through Europe.

1453 Ottoman Turks capture Constantinople, conquering the Byzantine Empire.

1492 Columbus arrives in North America.

1500s Reformers break away from the Catholic Church, and Protestantism is born.

1776 The U.S. Declaration of Independence is signed.

1789 The French Revolution begins.

Venezuelan History

Bolívar and his troops defeat the Spanish in the Battle of Carabobo; the Republic of Gran Colombia expands to unify Venezuela, Colombia, Ecuador, and Panama.	1821
Venezuela secedes from Gran Colombia and becomes a republic.	1830
José Antonio Páez is elected the first president of Venezuela.	1831
Juan Vicente Gómez becomes dictator of Venezuela.	1908
Venezuela's oil boom begins with the drilling of a well near Lake Maracaibo.	1922
A citizens' political party joins with the military to take control of the government.	1945
The military takes over the government following a coup.	1948
Civilian rule is reestablished.	1959
A new Venezuelan constitution is approved.	1961
The government nationalizes the petroleum industry.	1976
Falling oil prices begin the decline of Venezuela's economy.	1983
Hugo Chávez is elected president.	1998
Venezuela adopts a new constitution.	1999
A coup attempt against Hugo Chávez fails.	2002
Government reforms grant more power to the president.	2010

World History

1865	The American Civil War ends.
1879	The first practical lightbulb is invented.
1914	World War I begins.
1917	The Bolshevik Revolution brings communism to Russia.
1929	A worldwide economic depression begins.
1939	World War II begins.
1945	World War II ends.
1969	Humans land on the Moon.
1975	The Vietnam War ends.
1989	The Berlin Wall is torn down as communism crumbles in Eastern Europe.
1991	The Soviet Union breaks into separate states.
2001	Terrorists attack the World Trade Center in New York City and the Pentagon near Washington, D.C.
2004	A tsunami in the Indian Ocean destroys coastlines in Africa, India, and Southeast Asia.
2008	The United States elects its first African American president.

Fast Facts

Official name: Bolivarian Republic of Venezuela

Capital: Caracas

Official language: Spanish and many indigenous languages

Caracas

Venezuelan flag

Official religion:	None
Year of founding:	1811
National anthem:	*"Gloria al Bravo Pueblo"* ("Glory to the Brave People")
Type of government:	Federal republic
Head of state:	President
Head of government:	President
Area of country:	352,143 square miles (912,050 sq km)
Latitude and longitude of geographic center:	8° N, 66° W
Bordering countries:	Colombia to the west, Brazil to the south, and Guyana to the east
Highest elevation:	Bolívar Peak, 16,342 feet (4,981 m) above sea level
Lowest elevation:	Sea level along the coast
Highest average temperature:	85°F (29°C) in Maracaibo
Lowest average temperature:	65°F (18°C) in Caracas.
Average annual precipitation:	33 inches (84 cm) in Caracas; 23 inches (58 cm) in Maracaibo

Angel Falls

Roraima Tepui

National population (2010 est.):	29,044,000	
Population of major cities (2012 est.):	Caracas	6,000,000
	Maracaibo	1,891,800
	Valencia	1,408,400
	Barquisimeto	1,018,900
	Ciudad Guayana	789,500

Landmarks:
- ▶ *Angel Falls*, south of Ciudad Bolívar
- ▶ *Mérida cable car*, Mérida
- ▶ *National Art Gallery*, Caracas
- ▶ *Rafael Urdaneta Bridge*, Maracaibo
- ▶ *Roraima Tepui*, near the border with Brazil and Guyana

Economy: Oil is the main industry in Venezuela. Oil sales to other countries make up about 95 percent of all the money Venezuela brings in from its exports. Products being mined in Venezuela include iron ore, bauxite, and phosphate rock. Manufactured items include petroleum products, construction materials, processed foods, steel, textiles, and aluminum.

Currency: The bolívar fuerte. In June 2012, US$1.00 equaled 4.3 bolívares fuertes.

Currency

System of weights and measures: Metric system

Literacy rate (2006): 95 percent

Schoolchildren

Carolina Herrera

Common Spanish words and phrases:

Buenos días	Good morning
Buenas noches	Good evening
Hola, me llamo . . .	Hello, my name is . . .
Mucho gusto.	Nice to meet you.
Por favor	Please
Gracias	Thank you
De nada	You're welcome
Adiós	Good-bye

Prominent Venezuelans:

Hugo Chávez   (1954–)
President

Gustavo Dudamel   (1981–)
Conductor

Ozzie Guillen   (1964–)
Baseball player and manager

Carolina Herrera   (1939–)
Fashion designer

Francisco de Miranda   (1750–1816)
Revolutionary

Irene Sáez   (1961–)
Miss Universe and governor of Caracas

To Find Out More

Books

▶ Box, Ben. *Venezuela*. Bath, England: Footprint Handbooks, 2011.

▶ Crooker, Richard A. *Venezuela*. New York: Chelsea House Publications, 2006.

▶ Raub, Kevin, Brian Kluepfel, and Tom Masters. *Venezuela*. Oakland, CA: Lonely Planet, 2010.

Music

▶ Dudamel, Gustavo, and the Simón Bolívar Symphony Orchestra. *Fiesta*. Berlin, Germany: Deutsche Grammophon, 2008.

▶ *The Rough Guide to the Music of Venezuela*. London: World Music Network, 2003.

▶ Visit this Scholastic Web site for more information on Venezuela:
www.factsfornow.scholastic.com
Enter the keyword **Venezuela**

Index

Page numbers in *italics*
indicate illustrations.

Meet the Author

Terri Willis feels a special connection to Venezuela. Barquisimeto, Venezuela's fourth-largest city, is the home of a young woman her family sponsors. Over the years, Willis has heard from the young woman frequently, learning about her favorite classes and activities and the life she leads with her parents and brothers and sisters. Like so many others living in Venezuela, they are poor but hardworking. Willis says, "I thought about her often as I wrote this book. She was my inspiration. Her face reflects the diversity of the Venezuelan people, and her family's story of economic challenges mirrors the struggles of the country. She's hopeful that a good education will provide her with the opportunity to live a better life, a desire that's common not only to young people in Venezuela, but around the world. I have hopes for her, too, and the things I've learned while researching for this book have given me insight into what the future may hold for her generation of Venezuelans."

Willis graduated from the University of Wisconsin–Madison with a degree in journalism. She has edited and written books for young people for twenty years, focusing mostly on geographical, historical, and environmental top-

ics. Among the titles that she has written for Scholastic's Enchantment of the World series are *Afghanistan*, *Libya*, *The Democratic Republic of the Congo*, *Lebanon*, and *Vietnam*.

She and her husband, Harold, have two daughters, both in college. They live in Cedarburg, Wisconsin, where Willis also works as a substitute teacher. Middle-school students are her favorite. Anytime she is having difficulty writing about a particular topic, she thinks about how she would explain it to her favorite students. She tries to answer the questions they might ask and discuss the things they would find curious or amazing.

Photo Credits